PUGLIA TRA GUIDE 2024

DISCOVER THE HIDDEN PEARLS ,WONDEROUS ATTRACTION OF PUGLIA AND ITS ESSENTIAL TIPS.

MARIO ROCALLI

Table of contents

Introduction to Puglia

Welcome to Puglia, the captivating gem of Italy's southern coast! Nestled in the sun-kissed region of Apulia, this enchanting destination is a tapestry of history, culture, and natural beauty that will steal your heart from the moment you arrive. With its picturesque landscapes, charming coastal towns, and rich culinary traditions, Puglia is a true haven for those seeking an authentic Italian experience.

Imagine strolling along narrow cobblestone streets lined with whitewashed houses, their vibrant blue doors beckoning you to explore further. As you wander through the labyrinthine alleyways, the sweet aroma of freshly baked bread and aromatic olive oil fills the air, tempting your taste buds and awakening your senses. Puglia's culinary prowess is renowned, with its exquisite cuisine showcasing the region's bounty of fresh seafood, fragrant herbs, and sun-ripened produce. Beyond the tantalizing flavors, Puglia's landscapes are a sight to behold. From the iconic trulli houses of Alberobello, with their cone-shaped roofs, to the golden beaches that stretch as far as the eye can see, every corner of Puglia offers a postcard-worthy view.

History buffs will be captivated by Puglia's rich past, which dates back to ancient times. Explore the awe-inspiring archaeological sites of ancient Greek and Roman civilizations, such as the hauntingly beautiful ruins of Egnazia and the grandeur of the Roman Amphitheater in Lecce. Immerse yourself in the timeless charm of Ostuni's historic center, known as the "White City," or marvel at the ornate baroque architecture of Martina Franca. But Puglia is more than just a feast for the eyes and taste buds—it's a place that touches your soul. The warmth and hospitality of the locals will make you feel like family, and the vibrant festivals and lively music that fill the air will have you dancing to the rhythm of Puglia's heart. Whether you're sipping a glass of Primitivo wine in a traditional masseria, joining in the lively tarantella dance, or simply basking in the golden glow of the sunset over the olive groves, Puglia is a place where unforgettable memories are made.

So, come and immerse yourself in the captivating allure of Puglia. Let the magic of this southern Italian paradise embrace you, as you embark on a journey of discovery, indulgence, and pure joy. Puglia awaits, ready to unveil its wonders and leave an indelible mark on your heart.

Overview of Puglia

Welcome to Puglia, where dreams come alive amidst the sun-kissed landscapes and captivating charm of southern Italy. Nestled in the heart of the Mediterranean, Puglia beckons you with its irresistible allure and unforgettable experiences.

Puglia, known as the "heel of Italy's boot," is a treasure trove of hidden gems waiting to be discovered. From pristine white sandy beaches caressed by crystal-clear turquoise waters to picturesque countryside adorned with ancient olive groves and vineyards, this region is a feast for the senses.

Immerse yourself in the rich history and cultural heritage that permeates every corner of Puglia. Explore the enchanting trulli houses in Alberobello, a UNESCO World Heritage site, with their unique cone-shaped roofs that seem straight out of a fairytale. Meander through the narrow streets of Ostuni, the "White City," and marvel at its dazzling whitewashed buildings glistening under the Mediterranean sun. Indulge your taste buds with the delectable flavors of Puglia's renowned cuisine. Savor the velvety smoothness of extra virgin olive oil produced from centuries-old olive trees. Delight in the robust flavors of locally caught seafood, expertly prepared with traditional recipes passed down through generations. And, of course, don't miss the opportunity to sip on a glass of Primitivo or Negramaro, Puglia's prized wines that will transport you to vinous bliss. For the adventure seekers, Puglia offers a wealth of outdoor activities. Explore the dramatic coastline adorned with dramatic cliffs and hidden coves, perfect for snorkeling or diving into a world of underwater wonders. Take a leisurely bike ride through the rolling hills of the Itria Valley, dotted with charming villages and picturesque vineyards. Or simply bask in the Mediterranean sun on one of the region's stunning beaches, feeling the gentle sea breeze kiss your skin. Puglia's warmth extends beyond its sun-drenched landscapes; it lies within the hearts of its hospitable locals. Their genuine smiles and welcoming nature will make you feel like part of the family. Engage in lively conversations, learn traditional dances, and embrace the passionate spirit that defines Puglia's people. So, whether you seek relaxation, adventure, or a cultural awakening, Puglia is ready to captivate you with its unique blend of natural beauty, culinary delights, and heartfelt hospitality. Prepare to fall in love with a region that will leave an indelible mark on your soul. Welcome to Puglia, where dreams come true.

History and Culture

Puglia, also known as Apulia in English, is a region located in southern Italy. It occupies the "heel" of the Italian peninsula and is known for its rich history, diverse landscapes, and vibrant culture. Let's delve into the fascinating history and cultural heritage of Puglia.

History:

Puglia has a long and complex history that dates back to ancient times. The region was inhabited by various civilizations, including the Messapians, Greeks, Romans, Normans, and Byzantines. Each of these cultures left a lasting impact on the region's architecture, art, and traditions. During the ancient Greek period, several city-states were established in Puglia, such as Taranto and Brindisi. These cities thrived as important centers of trade and culture, leaving behind archaeological sites and artifacts that are still visible today. In the Roman era, Puglia became part of the Roman Republic and later the Roman Empire. The Romans built infrastructure, such as roads and aqueducts, which facilitated trade and communication throughout the region. Puglia's strategic location also made it a crucial outpost for the Roman Empire in its conflicts with other powers. In the medieval period, Puglia experienced significant Norman influence. The Normans, led by Robert Guiscard, conquered the region in the 11th century, bringing feudalism and a distinctive architectural style. The well-known Castel del Monte, a UNESCO World Heritage site, was built during this time and stands as a testament to Norman craftsmanship.

Culture:

Puglia's culture is a blend of diverse influences, reflecting its historical interactions with different civilizations. The region's culture is characterized by its cuisine, folk traditions, music, and festivals.

Cuisine: Puglia is renowned for its culinary delights, including fresh seafood, olive oil, pasta, and local wines. The region is the largest producer of olive oil in Italy, and its olive groves are a characteristic feature of the landscape. Local dishes such as orecchiette (a type of pasta), burrata cheese, and tiella (a savory pie) showcase the rich culinary heritage of Puglia.

Folk Traditions: Puglia has a vibrant tradition of folk dances, music, and costumes. The "Pizzica" is a traditional dance often associated with the region, accompanied by lively music played on instruments like tambourines and accordions. These folk traditions are often performed during festivals and celebrations, creating a sense of community and cultural pride.

Architecture: Puglia boasts a diverse architectural landscape. The trulli, traditional dry stone huts with conical roofs, are iconic to the region and can be found primarily in the town of Alberobello. These unique structures, also designated as a UNESCO World Heritage site, have become a symbol of Puglia's cultural identity.

Religious Sites: Puglia is home to numerous churches, cathedrals, and religious sites. The Basilica di San Nicola in Bari, dedicated to St. Nicholas, attracts pilgrims from around the world. Other notable religious landmarks include the Cathedral of Trani and the Castel del Monte, which blends elements of religious and military architecture.

Festivals: Puglia hosts a variety of festivals throughout the year that celebrate religious, cultural, and historical events. The "Cavalcata di Sant'Oronzo" in Lecce, the "Festival della Taranta" in Melpignano, and the "Processione dei Misteri" in Taranto are just a few examples of the vibrant festivals that showcase the region's traditions and heritage. Puglia's history and culture have shaped its identity as a captivating and diverse region in Italy.

Best Time to Visit

The best time to visit Puglia, a beautiful region located in southern Italy, depends on your preferences and the experiences you are seeking. Puglia enjoys a Mediterranean climate, characterized by hot summers and mild winters, but there are a few factors to consider when planning your visit.

Spring (April to June): Spring is a fantastic time to visit Puglia, especially from April to June. The weather is generally pleasant, with temperatures ranging from 18°C to 25°C (64°F to 77°F). The countryside is lush and vibrant, and you can witness the blooming of wildflowers, olive groves, and vineyards. It's an excellent time for outdoor activities like hiking, cycling, and exploring the charming towns and coastal areas.

Summer (July to August): If you enjoy warm weather and vibrant beach scenes, summer is the ideal time to visit Puglia. The temperatures during July and August can reach around 30°C to 35°C

(86°F to 95°F), and the region comes alive with festivals, lively beach clubs, and bustling nightlife. However, it's worth noting that popular tourist destinations might be crowded during this period, especially in August when many Italians take their summer vacations.

Autumn (September to October): Autumn in Puglia is another great time to visit, particularly in September and October. The weather remains warm and pleasant, with temperatures ranging from 20°C to 28°C (68°F to 82°F). The summer crowds begin to dissipate, making it a more tranquil and enjoyable time to explore the region. Autumn also brings grape harvest season, offering opportunities to participate in wine festivals and taste the renowned wines of Puglia.

Winter (November to March): Puglia experiences mild winters compared to other parts of Italy, with temperatures ranging from 10°C to 15°C (50°F to 59°F). While it may not be beach weather, winter can still be an appealing time to visit if you prefer quieter surroundings and want to experience the local culture and traditions. The region hosts various winter festivals and events, and you can enjoy exploring the historical sites, indulging in hearty local cuisine, and taking advantage of lower accommodation prices.

Ultimately, the best time to visit Puglia depends on your preferences, whether it's enjoying the warm summer sun, witnessing the countryside in bloom, or experiencing the region's cultural events. Consider the weather, crowd levels, and activities you wish to partake in to determine the ideal time for your visit to this enchanting part of Italy.

Getting to Puglia

Getting to Puglia, a stunning region located in the southern part of Italy, is an exciting journey filled with beautiful landscapes, historical sites, and delicious cuisine. Whether you're traveling from within Italy or from another country, there are several convenient options available to reach this charming destination.

By Air: The most convenient way to reach Puglia from abroad is by flying into one of the region's airports. The two main airports in Puglia are Bari Karol Wojtyla Airport (BRI) and Brindisi Airport (BDS). These airports are well-connected to major European cities, making it easy to find direct flights or convenient connections. From Bari or Brindisi airports, you can rent a car or take public transportation to reach your final destination within Puglia. Both airports offer car rental services, and there are also shuttle buses and taxis available outside the terminals. Bari airport is located closer to the northern part of Puglia, while Brindisi airport is more convenient for reaching the southern areas.

By Train: If you prefer to travel by train, Italy has an excellent railway network that connects major cities and regions, including Puglia. The cities of Bari and Brindisi are the main railway hubs in the region. There are high-speed trains, such as Frecciarossa and Frecciargento, that run from major Italian cities like Rome, Florence, and Milan to Bari and Brindisi. Once you arrive at Bari or Brindisi train stations, you can easily reach your desired destination within Puglia by taking local trains, regional buses, or renting a car. The regional train service, Ferrovie del Sud Est, connects various towns and cities in Puglia, making it convenient to explore the region at your own pace.

By Car: If you prefer the freedom of driving and exploring the countryside, traveling to Puglia by car can be a great option. Italy has a well-developed road network, and Puglia is accessible via the A14 and A16 highways. The journey from Rome to Puglia takes approximately 4-5 hours by car, while from Naples, it takes around 3-4 hours. Once you arrive in Puglia, there are several scenic routes to explore, such as the coastal road that runs along the Adriatic Sea or the inland routes that pass through picturesque countryside and charming towns.

By Ferry: Another unique way to reach Puglia is by taking a ferry. There are ferry connections between Puglia and Greece, with services operating from the ports of Bari and Brindisi. These ferries provide a memorable experience and offer an alternative way to arrive in Puglia if you're already in Greece or looking for a longer, more adventurous journey.

Puglia is a captivating region that offers a diverse range of experiences, from exploring ancient cities like Lecce and Alberobello with its famous trulli houses, to relaxing on beautiful beaches along the Adriatic or Ionian coasts. However you choose to travel, reaching Puglia is the beginning of an unforgettable adventure in one of Italy's most enchanting regions.

Karol Wojtyła Airport, which offers international and domestic flights. You can also consider flying into Brindisi Airport, especially if you plan to explore the southern part of the region. Another option is to take a train from major Italian cities like Rome or Naples.

Transportation: Renting a car is highly recommended in Puglia as it provides the most flexibility to explore the region. The road network is generally good, and driving allows you to visit smaller towns and picturesque countryside areas. Alternatively, you can use the efficient regional train network to get around, but it may limit your access to certain destinations.

Must-Visit Places: Puglia is known for its stunning coastal towns, charming villages, and unique architecture. Make sure to visit Alberobello, famous for its trulli houses; Ostuni, the "White City"; Lecce, known as the "Florence of the South" for its Baroque architecture; and Polignano a Mare, a picturesque seaside town. Don't miss the beautiful beaches of Salento, such as Porto Cesareo and Gallipoli.

Food and Wine: Puglia is a food lover's paradise, renowned for its fresh seafood, olive oil, and hearty cuisine. Try the local specialties like orecchiette pasta, burrata cheese, taralli (savory biscuits), and olio di oliva (olive oil). Puglia is also a significant wine region, producing excellent reds like Primitivo and Negroamaro. Take a wine tour and visit some of the region's vineyards for tastings.

Cultural Experiences: Puglia has a rich cultural heritage, and you can immerse yourself in its history by visiting the UNESCO World Heritage Sites like the trulli of Alberobello, the Castel del Monte, and the historic centers of Lecce and Matera (which is technically in the neighboring region of Basilicata). Attend local festivals, such as the Notte della Taranta, a traditional music festival held in various towns throughout the summer.

Beaches and Coastline: Puglia boasts a stunning coastline with crystal-clear waters. Explore the Gargano Peninsula, where you'll find beautiful beaches and the charming town of Vieste. Visit the Tremiti Islands for a more secluded beach experience. In the south, the Salento Peninsula offers picturesque coastal towns and Caribbean-like beaches, such as Baia dei Turchi and Punta Prosciutto.

Respect Local Customs: Italians, including the people of Puglia, appreciate polite behavior and dressing appropriately when visiting churches or religious sites. It's also customary to greet locals with a "buongiorno" (good morning) or "buonasera" (good evening) and to try a few Italian phrases, even if your language skills are limited.

Remember to check for any travel advisories or restrictions before your trip, and always follow local guidelines and regulations. Enjoy your visit to Puglia and soak up the beauty, history, and delicious cuisine the region has to offer!

Exploring Puglia's Coastal Gems

Bari: The Gateway to Puglia

Bari: The Gateway to Puglia Situated on the Adriatic coast of southern Italy, Bari serves as the gateway to the beautiful region of Puglia. With its rich history, charming old town, vibrant culture, and stunning coastline, Bari has become a popular destination for travelers seeking an authentic Italian experience. Bari's most famous attraction is its historic center, known as Bari Vecchia. Stepping into this maze-like district feels like stepping back in time. Narrow winding streets, whitewashed houses with colorful shutters, and hanging laundry create a picturesque setting that captures the essence of traditional southern Italian life. As you explore Bari Vecchia, you'll encounter charming piazzas, ancient churches, and hidden courtyards, each with its own story to tell. One of the main highlights of Bari Vecchia is the Basilica di San Nicola, dedicated to Saint Nicholas, the patron saint of the city. This impressive Romanesque church houses the relics of Saint Nicholas and attracts pilgrims from around the world. Its stunning architecture and intricate details make it a must-visit for history and art enthusiasts. Bari is also known for its vibrant food scene, showcasing the flavors of Puglia. The city's bustling markets, such as Mercato Coperto and Mercato del Pesce, offer a sensory feast of fresh seafood, locally grown fruits and vegetables, and aromatic spices. Don't miss the opportunity to try some of the region's culinary delights, including orecchiette pasta, burrata cheese, and seafood dishes like tiella and frittura di paranza.

For a breath of fresh air, head to Bari's waterfront promenade, known as Lungomare Nazario Sauro. Here, you can enjoy a leisurely stroll along the Adriatic Sea, take in the beautiful views, and relax at one of the many cafes and restaurants lining the promenade. Bari's beaches, such as Pane e Pomodoro and Torre Quetta, offer a perfect spot to soak up the sun and enjoy the crystal-clear waters of the Adriatic. Beyond the city limits, Bari serves as a convenient starting point for exploring the enchanting region of Puglia. Within a short drive, you can discover picturesque towns like Alberobello with its iconic trulli houses, the baroque beauty of Lecce, the whitewashed charm of Ostuni, and the stunning coastal landscapes of Polignano a Mare. Whether you're captivated by its history, enticed by its cuisine, or charmed by its coastal beauty, Bari truly is the gateway to Puglia. It invites you to immerse yourself in the authentic Italian lifestyle, experience the warmth of its people, and create unforgettable memories in one of Italy's most captivating regions

Lecce: The Baroque Beauty

Lecce, known as the "Baroque Beauty" of Puglia, is a charming city located in the southern region of Italy. With its rich history, stunning architecture, and vibrant culture, Lecce offers visitors a unique and unforgettable experience. One of the most captivating aspects of Lecce is its Baroque architecture, which dominates the cityscape. The use of local limestone, known as "Lecce stone," gives the buildings a warm golden hue, creating a magical ambiance. As you stroll through the narrow streets, you'll be mesmerized by the intricate details adorning the facades of churches, palaces, and public squares. The Basilica di Santa Croce stands as a masterpiece of Baroque architecture, featuring ornate carvings, delicate statues, and a magnificent rose window.

Lecce's historic center, often referred to as the "Florence of the South," is a UNESCO World Heritage site. It is a labyrinth of narrow alleyways and hidden courtyards, where every turn reveals a new architectural gem. Piazza del Duomo is the heart of the city, with its elegant cathedral and the Campanile, offering breathtaking panoramic views. Nearby, Piazza Sant'Oronzo is a vibrant square where you can admire the remains of the ancient Roman amphitheater, which has become a symbol of the city. Beyond its architectural splendors, Lecce is a city of art and culture. The city is home to numerous art galleries, museums, and artisan workshops, where you can discover the rich artistic traditions of the region. The craftsmanship of the local artisans is particularly renowned for its papier-mâché creations, which range from intricate masks to decorative figurines. Exploring the workshops and witnessing the creation process is a fascinating experience.

Lecce is also a culinary delight, offering a wide array of traditional dishes that showcase the flavors of Puglia. The local cuisine is based on simple, fresh ingredients, with a focus on olive oil, vegetables, and seafood. Don't miss the opportunity to taste the famous Pasticciotto, a sweet pastry filled with custard, or indulge in a plate of orecchiette, the region's signature pasta shape. During the summer months, Lecce comes alive with festivals and events celebrating its cultural heritage. The Lecce Baroque Festival showcases music and performances in stunning Baroque settings, while the Festa di Sant'Oronzo honors the city's patron saint with a vibrant parade and fireworks. Surrounded by the beautiful countryside of the Salento region, Lecce also offers access to stunning beaches and picturesque coastal towns. The crystal-clear waters of the Ionian and Adriatic Seas beckon visitors to relax and unwind, while the nearby towns of Gallipoli, Otranto, and Ostuni are perfect for day trips.

Lecce, with its Baroque beauty, artistic treasures, and warm hospitality, is a destination that captivates the hearts of all who visit. Whether you are an art enthusiast, a history buff, a food lover, or simply in search of a charming and authentic Italian experience, Lecce is sure to leave a lasting impression

Polignano a Mare: Cliffs and Caves

Polignano a Mare is a breathtaking coastal town located in the southern region of Puglia, Italy. Renowned for its dramatic cliffs and mesmerizing caves, it offers visitors a unique and unforgettable experience. Situated atop limestone cliffs that overlook the crystal-clear Adriatic Sea, Polignano a Mare boasts some of the most picturesque and dramatic coastal landscapes in Italy. The town's cliffs are a natural wonder, rising majestically from the sea, creating a stunning backdrop for the charming white-washed houses that dot the shoreline. One of the highlights of Polignano a Mare is its incredible network of caves. Carved by the relentless force of the sea over thousands of years, these caves showcase nature's artistic prowess. The most famous among them is the Grotta Palazzese, an enchanting cave restaurant nestled within a large sea cave. Dining at the Grotta Palazzese is a truly unique experience, as you savor delicious local cuisine while surrounded by the dramatic cave walls and the sound of crashing waves. Another noteworthy cave is the Grotta Ardito, which can be accessed by boat or by descending a staircase from the town's main square. This cave is known for its striking blue waters, which are illuminated by sunlight filtering through an opening in the cave ceiling. The Grotta Ardito offers a tranquil and magical atmosphere, perfect for those seeking a moment of serenity.

For the adventurous souls, exploring the caves by boat or kayak is a must. Guided tours are available, allowing visitors to delve into the hidden corners of these natural wonders. As you navigate through the labyrinthine caves, you'll be captivated by the intricate rock formations and the interplay of light and shadow. Aside from the cliffs and caves, Polignano a Mare has much more to offer. Its historic center is a labyrinth of narrow streets, charming squares, and picturesque viewpoints that provide panoramic vistas of the coastline. Take a leisurely stroll through the town, and you'll discover hidden gems at every turn, including quaint shops, traditional restaurants, and vibrant cafés.

In addition to its natural beauty, Polignano a Mare is also known for its cultural events and festivals. The Red Bull Cliff Diving World Series takes place here, attracting daredevil divers who leap from the cliffs into the sea below, showcasing their incredible skills and defying gravity. Whether you're an adventure seeker, a nature lover, or a culture enthusiast, Polignano a Mare is a destination that will leave you in awe. Its majestic cliffs and captivating caves create an atmosphere of wonder and enchantment, making it a must-visit place for anyone exploring the beautiful region of Puglia

Otranto: Coastal Splendor

Nestled on the picturesque Adriatic coast of southern Italy, Otranto stands as a beacon of coastal splendor in the region of Puglia. With its breathtaking scenery, rich history, and charming ambiance, Otranto captivates visitors with its unique blend of natural beauty and cultural heritage. One of the first things that strikes you when you arrive in Otranto is the sheer beauty of its coastline. Crystal-clear turquoise waters gently lap against pristine sandy beaches, inviting visitors to unwind and soak up the Mediterranean sun. The dramatic cliffs that line the shore create a striking contrast against the azure sea, adding to the area's allure. The panoramic views from the coastal promenade are simply awe-inspiring, offering a glimpse of the ethereal beauty that awaits.

Beyond its stunning coastline, Otranto boasts a captivating history that dates back centuries. The town's historical center, enclosed within ancient walls, exudes an enchanting atmosphere. Stepping into the labyrinthine streets feels like stepping back in time, as you wander through narrow alleyways adorned with colorful flowers and traditional stone houses. The crown jewel of Otranto's historical center is the magnificent Cathedral, a UNESCO World Heritage Site. Its intricate mosaic floor, known as the Tree of Life, is a true masterpiece that narrates biblical stories and mythical creatures. Exploring the cathedral is a mesmerizing experience that unveils the town's rich cultural heritage.

As you venture further into Otranto's historical past, you'll encounter the imposing Aragonese Castle. Built in the 15th century to protect the town from invasions, the castle now serves as a museum, offering a glimpse into Otranto's tumultuous history. Its fortified walls, imposing towers, and breathtaking views of the Adriatic Sea make it a must-visit destination for history enthusiasts and those seeking to immerse themselves in the region's storied past.

In addition to its natural beauty and historical treasures, Otranto is also a culinary delight. Puglia, known as the "breadbasket of Italy," offers a rich and diverse gastronomy, and Otranto showcases the region's culinary prowess. Indulge in freshly caught seafood, fragrant olive oils, locally produced wines, and delectable pastries that showcase the flavors of the Mediterranean. The town's restaurants and trattorias offer a delightful blend of traditional and innovative dishes, providing a true feast for the senses. For those seeking outdoor adventures, Otranto offers a myriad of activities to satisfy every taste. From boat trips along the stunning coastline to hiking and biking excursions in the nearby countryside, there's no shortage of ways to connect with nature and explore the area's natural wonders. Whether you prefer to relax on the beach, embark on a snorkeling adventure, or simply take a leisurely stroll along the promenade, Otranto offers a diverse range of options for outdoor enthusiasts.

Otranto is a hidden gem on Italy's Adriatic coast, a coastal paradise that seamlessly blends history, natural beauty, and culinary delights. Whether you're drawn to its pristine beaches, mesmerized by its historical landmarks, or simply eager to savor the flavors of Puglia, Otranto promises an unforgettable experience. Immerse yourself in its coastal splendor, and you'll discover a destination that captivates the heart and soul, leaving you with memories to cherish for a lifetime

Monopoli: Charming Seaside Town

Monopoli, a charming seaside town located in the picturesque region of Puglia in southern Italy, is a hidden gem that captivates visitors with its beauty, history, and laid-back atmosphere. Nestled along the Adriatic Sea, Monopoli is renowned for its stunning beaches, ancient architecture, and delectable cuisine, making it a perfect destination for those seeking an authentic Italian experience. One of the most alluring aspects of Monopoli is its enchanting historic center. The town's labyrinthine alleys are lined with whitewashed buildings adorned with vibrant flowers, creating a postcard-worthy scene at every turn. Exploring the narrow streets, visitors will stumble upon charming squares, quaint churches, and hidden courtyards, each with its own story to tell. The imposing Monopoli Cathedral, dedicated to the Assumption of the Virgin Mary, stands as a prominent landmark and showcases the town's rich history.

Monopoli's coastal beauty is another major draw for tourists. With its crystal-clear turquoise waters, secluded coves, and sandy beaches, the town offers a paradise-like setting for sunbathing, swimming, and water sports. The iconic Cala Porta Vecchia beach, nestled beneath the ancient city walls, provides a breathtaking backdrop for relaxation and leisure. Visitors can also explore the picturesque harbor, where colorful fishing boats bob in the water, and enjoy a leisurely stroll along the promenade while savoring the fresh sea breeze.

For history enthusiasts, Monopoli offers a glimpse into its storied past through its impressive architecture and historical landmarks. The 16th-century Castle of Charles V, once a defensive fortress, now houses exhibitions and cultural events that provide insight into the town's heritage. Another must-visit site is the Palmieri Palace, a grand mansion that showcases the opulence of Monopoli's noble families. Culinary delights await visitors in Monopoli, as the town is renowned for its exceptional cuisine. Fresh seafood takes center stage on menus, with dishes like octopus salad, grilled fish, and seafood pasta being local favorites. Monopoli's restaurants also serve up traditional Puglian delicacies such as orecchiette pasta, burrata cheese, and focaccia, all of which can be paired with the region's excellent wines.

Throughout the year, Monopoli hosts various cultural events and festivals that add vibrancy and charm to the town. The Feast of the Madonna della Madia, held in August, is a religious celebration featuring a spectacular procession and fireworks. The Jazz Festival, attracting renowned musicians from around the world, is another highlight for music lovers.

In addition to its own attractions, Monopoli serves as an excellent base for exploring the wider region of Puglia. The nearby towns of Alberobello, known for its iconic trulli houses, and Polignano a Mare, with its stunning cliffside views, are just a short drive away. Visitors can also venture further inland to discover the enchanting landscapes of the Valle d'Itria or explore the baroque beauty of Lecce. With its irresistible combination of history, natural beauty, and gastronomic delights, Monopoli offers a truly authentic Italian experience. Whether you're seeking relaxation on sun-kissed beaches, a journey through history and culture, or simply a taste of the renowned Puglian cuisine, this charming seaside town will leave you spellbound and longing to return

Gallipoli: The Ionian Gem in puglia:

Introduction:

Nestled on the sun-kissed shores of the Ionian Sea in the southern Italian region of Puglia, Gallipoli is a true hidden gem that captivates visitors with its picturesque beauty, rich history, and vibrant culture. This enchanting coastal town, known as "Gallipoli La Bella" (Gallipoli the Beautiful), offers a perfect blend of stunning beaches, ancient architecture, delectable cuisine, and warm hospitality. Let us embark on a journey to explore the allure of Gallipoli and discover why it is hailed as the Ionian Gem of Puglia.

Historical Significance:

Gallipoli's history dates back to ancient times when it was a thriving Greek colony known as "Kallipolis" (Beautiful City). Over the centuries, it has witnessed the rise and fall of various civilizations, including the Greeks, Romans, Byzantines, and Normans. The town's strategic location on a limestone island connected to the mainland by a 17th-century bridge made it a coveted stronghold for many powers throughout history. The imposing walls, forts, and watchtowers that dot the town's landscape stand as a testament to its turbulent past.

Charming Old Town: Gallipoli's heart lies within its captivating Old Town, an intricate maze of narrow cobblestone streets, whitewashed buildings adorned with colorful flower pots, and charming squares bustling with life. Stroll through the labyrinthine alleys and discover hidden gems at every turn, from picturesque churches like the stunning Cathedral of Sant'Agata to the awe-inspiring Angevin Castle. The medieval architecture and well-preserved historical buildings create an ambiance that transports visitors back in time.

Sun-Kissed Beaches: Gallipoli's real treasure lies in its sun-drenched beaches and crystal-clear turquoise waters. The Ionian Coast boasts some of the most pristine and inviting beaches in Italy, and Gallipoli is no exception. Lido San Giovanni and

Baia Verde are two popular beach destinations that offer stretches of soft golden sand, beach clubs, and refreshing sea breezes. Whether you prefer to relax on a sun lounger or dive into the refreshing waters, Gallipoli's beaches are sure to enchant beach lovers and water enthusiasts alike.

Culinary Delights: No visit to Gallipoli is complete without indulging in its mouthwatering cuisine. As a coastal town, it is renowned for its fresh seafood delicacies. Taste the catch of the day at one of the charming seafood trattorias, where you can savor dishes like "frittura di paranza" (mixed fried seafood) or "riso, patate e cozze" (rice, potatoes, and mussels). Don't miss the opportunity to pair your meal with a glass of the local Primitivo wine, known for its robust flavor and rich aroma.

Festivals and Vibrant Culture: Gallipoli comes alive with vibrant festivals and cultural events throughout the year. One of the most famous is the Feast of Sant'Agata, the town's patron saint, celebrated in early February. The streets are illuminated, and processions fill the air with a joyous atmosphere. Music festivals, art exhibitions, and traditional folk performances also take place, showcasing the region's cultural heritage and artistic talents.

Conclusion:

Gallipoli, the Ionian Gem in Puglia, offers a captivating blend of history, natural beauty, and authentic Italian charm. With its ancient treasures, sun-kissed beaches, delectable cuisine, and vibrant culture, this coastal town invites visitors to immerse themselves in its timeless allure. Whether you're seeking a relaxing beach getaway, a journey through history

Uncovering Puglia's Historic Treasures

Alberobello: Trulli Magic in puglia:

Nestled in the picturesque region of Puglia in southern Italy, Alberobello stands as a mesmerizing testament to a unique architectural heritage. This charming town is renowned for its enchanting trulli, traditional dry-stone huts with cone-shaped roofs that dot the landscape and create an otherworldly atmosphere. Alberobello's trulli have captivated visitors for centuries, drawing them into a world of magic and charm.

The trulli of Alberobello date back to the 14th century, and their origin is steeped in folklore and legend. According to popular belief, these peculiar structures were built without the use of mortar to allow the local population to dismantle them quickly in order to evade taxes imposed by the Kingdom of Naples. The cylindrical walls and conical roofs are constructed with local limestone, skillfully stacked in a way that creates stability without the need for cement or mortar.

Walking through the narrow streets of Alberobello feels like stepping into a fairy tale. The trulli line the winding alleys, adorned with whitewashed walls and symbols painted on the roofs. These symbols often feature religious or superstitious motifs, serving as a form of decoration and protection against evil spirits. One of the most remarkable features of the trulli is their exceptional thermal insulation. The limestone walls keep the interiors cool during hot summers and warm during chilly winters, providing natural climate control that is still effective today. Stepping inside a trullo, visitors are transported to a bygone era, where simplicity and functionality merge seamlessly. Alberobello's trulli have not only survived the test of time but have also been recognized as a UNESCO World Heritage site since 1996. This designation has preserved the town's unique character and ensured the conservation of its architectural treasures for generations to come.

Today, many of the trulli in Alberobello have been converted into shops, restaurants, and guest accommodations, allowing visitors to experience the magic of living in these historic dwellings. Exploring the town's trulli district, known as Rione Monti, is an unforgettable experience, as every corner reveals new surprises and delights.

In addition to its architectural wonders, Alberobello offers a wealth of cultural and culinary experiences. Visitors can immerse themselves in the local traditions, tasting the delicious Apulian cuisine, characterized by fresh seafood, locally grown vegetables, and renowned olive oil. The town also hosts various festivals and events throughout the year, celebrating its rich heritage and captivating visitors with music, dancing, and vibrant displays of local customs.

Alberobello's trulli are a testament to human ingenuity and creativity, exemplifying the harmonious coexistence between man and nature. Their whimsical beauty and unique construction make this small town in Puglia a must-visit destination for those seeking a truly enchanting experience. Whether you wander through the narrow streets, savor the local flavors, or simply bask in the ambiance of the trulli, Alberobello promises an unforgettable journey into a world of trulli magic

Castel del Monte:

Castel del Monte, located in the stunning region of Puglia in southern Italy, is an architectural marvel that has captivated visitors for centuries. This unique and enigmatic castle stands atop a hill in the countryside, overlooking the surrounding landscape with an air of mystery and intrigue. It is renowned for its striking octagonal shape, harmonious proportions, and intricate design, which blend various architectural styles into a masterpiece of medieval architecture. Commissioned by the Holy Roman Emperor Frederick II in the 13th century, Castel del Monte was intended to serve as a hunting lodge and a symbol of imperial power. Its construction began around 1240 and continued over several decades, resulting in a structure that defies categorization. The castle is a blend of influences, combining elements of Romanesque, Gothic, and Islamic architecture, reflecting the diverse cultural heritage of its creator.

The octagonal shape of Castel del Monte is its defining feature, with each of its eight sides carefully designed to create a sense of symmetry and balance. The exterior is adorned with delicate stone decorations, including intricate carvings, geometric patterns, and reliefs. The simplicity of the design, characterized by minimal ornamentation and clean lines, emphasizes the castle's geometric precision and understated elegance. Inside, the castle's layout is equally fascinating. The ground floor consists of eight chambers, each connected to the central courtyard, while the upper floor houses an octagonal gallery. The interior spaces are adorned with exquisite details, such as marble floors, sculpted capitals, and intricately carved fireplaces. The vaulted ceilings, supported by elegant columns, add to the overall grandeur of the castle. One of the enduring mysteries surrounding Castel del Monte is its purpose and symbolic significance. The octagonal shape has been subject to numerous theories and interpretations, ranging from astrological symbolism to connections with the Emperor's intellectual pursuits. Its remote location, distant from any major cities or trade routes, adds to the enigmatic aura surrounding the castle.

Despite its historical significance and architectural brilliance, Castel del Monte fell into neglect over the centuries, and its original furnishings were lost or destroyed. However, in the 19th century, efforts were made to restore and preserve this extraordinary structure. In 1996, UNESCO designated Castel del Monte as a World Heritage Site, recognizing its cultural value and its status as a unique architectural gem.

Today, visitors can explore the castle's interior, marvel at its architectural splendor, and soak in the panoramic views of the Apulian countryside from its elevated position. The site also hosts cultural events and exhibitions that shed light on its rich history and architectural legacy.

Castel del Monte stands as a testament to the genius of Frederick II and the remarkable fusion of architectural styles that emerged during the Middle

Ages. Its geometric precision, elegant simplicity, and enigmatic charm continue to captivate visitors, making it a must-visit destination for architecture enthusiasts, history buffs, and curious travelers exploring the wonders of Puglia.

Matera: Cave Dwellings and Sassi

Matera is a captivating city located in the region of Basilicata, in southern Italy. Renowned for its ancient cave dwellings and unique urban landscape, Matera is a UNESCO World Heritage site and a fascinating destination for history enthusiasts and curious travelers alike.

The heart of Matera's allure lies in its ancient districts known as "Sassi." The Sassi di Matera are a complex network of cave dwellings, churches, and narrow streets carved into the soft tufa rock. These dwellings have been inhabited continuously for thousands of years, making them one of the oldest human settlements in Italy and Europe.

The Sassi can be divided into two main areas: Sasso Caveoso and Sasso Barisano. Sasso Caveoso is the older of the two and is characterized by its rugged and irregular structures. Walking through its winding streets, visitors can explore ancient cave houses, churches, and even rock-cut cisterns that were once used to collect rainwater. The architecture of the Sasso Caveoso reflects a rich history of different civilizations, including the Greeks, Romans, Byzantines, and Lombards, all of whom left their mark on the city. Sasso Barisano, on the other hand, showcases a more organized and urban layout. Here, visitors can find a mix of cave dwellings and more conventional buildings, with narrow lanes and staircases connecting the different levels. Some of the caves have been transformed into charming hotels, restaurants, and shops, offering a unique experience for those looking to immerse themselves in Matera's history. One of the most iconic sights in Matera is the Church of San Pietro Caveoso, located in the Sasso Caveoso. This ancient church dates back to the 12th century and is partially carved into the rock, with a fascinating blend of architectural styles. Its interior features beautiful frescoes and religious artifacts that provide a glimpse into Matera's religious heritage.

In recent years, Matera has undergone a significant transformation, shedding its reputation as a poverty-stricken area. The city has been revitalized, and the cave dwellings have been restored, turning some of them into museums and cultural centers. Matera was also chosen as the European Capital of Culture in 2019, further elevating its status and attracting a larger number of visitors from around the world.

Exploring Matera and its Sassi is like stepping back in time. The unique combination of history, architecture, and natural beauty creates an enchanting atmosphere that captivates visitors. As you wander through the narrow alleys and discover hidden caves and courtyards, you'll feel the weight of centuries of human existence and appreciate the resilience of the Materans who have made this place their home for millennia.

In conclusion, Matera's cave dwellings and Sassi are an extraordinary testament to human ingenuity and endurance. They provide an unparalleled glimpse into the ancient past while showcasing the remarkable ability of a community to adapt and thrive within a challenging environment. A visit to Matera is a journey into history, culture, and the incredible spirit of this captivating city in the Puglia region of Italy

Ostuni: The White City

Ostuni, often referred to as the "White City," is a breathtaking destination located in the region of Puglia, in southern Italy. With its picturesque architecture, dazzling white buildings, and rich cultural heritage, Ostuni attracts visitors from around the world. Perched atop a hill overlooking the Adriatic Sea, Ostuni is renowned for its distinctive appearance. The city's historic center is a maze of narrow, winding streets lined with whitewashed houses, creating a striking contrast against the vibrant blue sky. The whitewashing tradition dates back centuries and serves both practical and aesthetic purposes. The lime wash used to paint the buildings not only reflects sunlight, keeping the interiors cool during the hot summer months but also gives Ostuni its signature luminous and magical ambiance.

Exploring Ostuni's historic center is like stepping into a fairytale. As you stroll through the labyrinthine streets, you'll discover charming alleys adorned with colorful flowers, quaint squares where locals gather, and hidden corners that beckon you to wander further. The city's architecture showcases a fusion of influences, from medieval to Baroque, providing a captivating glimpse into its past. One of Ostuni's most iconic landmarks is the Cathedral of Santa Maria Assunta. Built in the 15th century, the cathedral boasts an impressive façade adorned with rose windows, intricate carvings, and a towering campanile. Inside, visitors can admire beautiful frescoes and a serene atmosphere that invites contemplation.

Beyond its architectural wonders, Ostuni offers a vibrant cultural scene. The city hosts numerous festivals and events throughout the year, celebrating traditions, music, and local cuisine. Don't miss the "Cavalcata di Sant'Oronzo" held in August, a lively parade honoring the city's patron saint, which brings together locals dressed in traditional costumes, vibrant floats, and spirited horse riders. Ostuni is also a culinary delight. Puglia, known as the "breadbasket of Italy," is renowned for its gastronomy, and Ostuni is no exception. Indulge in the region's famous olive oil, freshly baked bread, handmade pasta, and succulent seafood dishes. The city's charming trattorias and restaurants offer a wide array of culinary delights that will satisfy even the most discerning palate.

Nature lovers will appreciate Ostuni's proximity to the stunning coastline of the Adriatic Sea. Just a short drive away, you'll find pristine beaches, crystal-clear waters, and hidden coves framed by rugged cliffs. Take a dip in the refreshing sea, soak up the sun, or explore the nearby nature reserves that showcase Puglia's unique flora and fauna.

Whether you're captivated by its dazzling architecture, immersed in its rich history, tantalized by its culinary treasures, or simply enchanted by its beauty, Ostuni, the White City, offers an unforgettable experience. Its timeless allure and warm hospitality make it a must-visit destination for travelers seeking an authentic taste of Italy's cultural and natural wonders

Trani: Ancient Seaport

Trani, an ancient seaport located in the beautiful region of Puglia, Italy, is a captivating destination that carries a rich historical and cultural heritage. This coastal town, situated on the Adriatic Sea, has been enchanting visitors for centuries with its picturesque setting, stunning architecture, and vibrant atmosphere. Trani's history dates back to ancient times when it was known as Turenum. It flourished during the Roman era as a crucial trade center, connecting the Adriatic Sea with the Mediterranean. Trani's strategic location made it an essential hub for maritime commerce, and its port thrived as a bustling trading post. One of the most remarkable landmarks in Trani is the Trani Cathedral, also known as the Cathedral of Saint Nicholas the Pilgrim. This imposing Romanesque structure stands proudly on the waterfront, showcasing its elegant white stone facade and impressive rose window. Built in the 12th century, the cathedral is a testament to Trani's medieval past and is considered one of the finest examples of Apulian Romanesque architecture.

Strolling through the streets of Trani's historic center, you'll encounter a myriad of narrow alleys, charming squares, and picturesque houses. The old town, with its white limestone buildings and traditional architecture, exudes a timeless charm that transports you back in time. The medieval Jewish quarter, known as Giudecca, is another fascinating area to explore, offering a glimpse into Trani's multicultural past. The Trani harbor is a captivating place to spend time, surrounded by colorful fishing boats and lined with waterfront restaurants and cafes. Indulge in the local seafood delicacies, such as fresh oysters and delicious fish dishes, while enjoying the soothing sound of waves crashing against the harbor walls. This is also an excellent spot to witness breathtaking sunsets over the Adriatic Sea. For those seeking cultural experiences, Trani offers several museums and historical sites worth visiting. The Diocesan Museum displays a remarkable collection of religious art, including precious medieval artifacts and stunning religious paintings. The Swabian Castle, built by Emperor Frederick II in the 13th century, stands as a testament to Trani's strategic importance during the Middle Ages. Trani's beauty extends beyond its architectural wonders and historical sites. The town boasts a sandy beach where visitors can relax and soak up the Mediterranean sun. Whether you want to take a dip in the crystal-clear waters, go for a leisurely stroll along the promenade, or simply enjoy the beachside atmosphere, Trani offers a delightful coastal experience.

In addition to its cultural and natural attractions, Trani hosts various events and festivals throughout the year, showcasing the region's traditions and local customs. The Feast of St. Nicholas the Pilgrim, celebrated in May, is a highlight, featuring processions, music, and fireworks that bring the town to life. Trani, with its ancient seafaring history, architectural treasures, and coastal charm, offers visitors a unique and captivating experience.

Whether you are a history enthusiast, a lover of art and architecture, or simply seeking a peaceful seaside getaway, Trani in Puglia will undoubtedly leave an indelible mark on your heart and soul

Taranto: Ancient Greek Heritage in puglia:

Nestled along the coast of the southern Italian region of Puglia, the city of Taranto boasts a rich history that stretches back thousands of years. Once a flourishing Greek colony known as Taras, it became one of the most important centers of Magna Graecia, the Greek colonies established in southern Italy. Today, Taranto stands as a testament to its ancient Greek heritage, with numerous archaeological sites and cultural treasures that evoke the city's illustrious past. The foundation of Taras can be traced back to the 8th century BCE when Greek settlers from Sparta and other Greek city-states arrived on the shores of what is now modern-day Taranto. These colonists established a thriving city, strategically positioned on a natural harbor known as the Mar Grande, which provided them with access to the Mediterranean Sea and facilitated trade and cultural exchange with other Greek cities. The ancient Greeks bestowed upon

Taranto a remarkable architectural and cultural legacy. One of the most prominent archaeological sites in the city is the Taranto National Archaeological Museum, which houses an impressive collection of artifacts from the ancient Greek and Roman periods. The museum showcases exquisite pottery, statues, jewelry, and other objects that offer insights into the daily lives, religious practices, and artistic achievements of the ancient inhabitants of Taras.

At the heart of the ancient city lies the Aragonese Castle, a fortress that dominates the landscape and serves as a symbol of Taranto's history. Originally built by the Greeks and later expanded by the Romans and the Byzantines, the castle witnessed centuries of conflicts and power struggles. Today, visitors can explore its halls and ramparts, immersing themselves in the turbulent past of Taranto while enjoying panoramic views of the city and the sea. Another iconic site in Taranto is the Ancient Greek Theater, which was constructed in the 3rd century BCE. Carved into the natural slope of a hill, this well-preserved amphitheater once hosted dramatic performances and communal gatherings. Today, it stands as a magnificent reminder of the city's cultural vibrancy during the ancient Greek era. The old town of Taranto, known as the Città Vecchia, is a labyrinth of narrow streets and picturesque alleys that exude an old-world charm. Here, visitors can wander through the historic quarters, discovering ancient churches, traditional homes, and hidden courtyards. The San Cataldo Cathedral, with its mix of architectural styles ranging from Romanesque to Baroque, is a must-visit landmark in the Città Vecchia.

Beyond its archaeological treasures, Taranto also offers breathtaking coastal scenery. The Mar Piccolo, a small inland sea connected to the Mar Grande, provides a picturesque backdrop with its shimmering blue waters and dotted islands. Visitors can take leisurely boat trips to explore the islands, indulge in fresh seafood at waterfront restaurants, or simply soak in the serene beauty of the coastline. Taranto's ancient Greek heritage remains an integral part of its identity, and the city continues to celebrate its cultural roots through various festivals and events. The Taranto International Archaeological Film Festival, held annually, showcases documentaries and films that delve into the world of archaeology, history, and ancient civilizations, further enhancing the appreciation for the city's rich past.

Taranto's connection to its ancient Greek heritage is a testament to the enduring influence of ancient civilizations on modern society. Whether exploring its archaeological sites, strolling through its historic streets, or savoring its coastal beauty, visitors to Taranto can immerse themselves in the captivating legacy of Magna Graecia and experience a vibrant blend of past and present

Culinary Delights of Puglia

Pugliese Cuisine: A Gastronomic Journey

Puglia, located in the southern region of Italy, is a place where culinary traditions run deep and the love for food is celebrated in every bite. Pugliese cuisine, also known as Apulian cuisine, is a true gastronomic journey that takes you through a rich tapestry of flavors, fresh ingredients, and time-honored recipes. Let's embark on this delicious adventure and explore the highlights of Pugliese cuisine. One of the defining characteristics of Pugliese cuisine is its simplicity. The dishes are often prepared with just a handful of ingredients, allowing the flavors to shine through. Olive oil, a staple of the region, is used abundantly in almost every recipe, adding a distinctive touch to the dishes. Puglia's coastal location provides an abundance of seafood, which plays a significant role in the local cuisine. From the delicate octopus salads to the hearty fish soups, the flavors of the Adriatic and Ionian Seas are prominently featured.

One iconic dish is "riso, patate e cozze" (rice, potatoes, and mussels), where the sweetness of mussels combines with the creaminess of potatoes and the fragrant rice, creating a harmonious blend of flavors. Moving away from the coast, Puglia's fertile land offers a variety of fresh produce. The region is known as the "breadbasket of Italy" due to its vast olive groves, vineyards, and fields of durum wheat. The bread of Puglia, such as the famous Altamura bread, is legendary for its rustic crust and soft, airy interior. It is perfect for sopping up the delicious sauces and olive oil-based dishes that are abundant in the region.

Puglia is also renowned for its pasta. Orecchiette, meaning "little ears," is the most typical pasta shape of the region. Traditionally handmade by local women, these small, round pasta shells are served with various sauces. One classic preparation is "orecchiette con le cime di rapa," a dish featuring bitter greens known as broccoli rabe, sautéed with garlic and chili flakes, and tossed with the pasta. It's a simple yet satisfying dish that captures the essence of Pugliese cuisine.

Puglia is also the land of fantastic cheeses. Burrata, a creamy cheese made from mozzarella and cream, hails from the region. Served fresh and often accompanied by sun-ripened tomatoes, basil, and a drizzle of olive oil, burrata is a culinary delight that embodies the simplicity and quality of Pugliese cuisine. No journey through Puglia's culinary landscape would be complete without indulging in its sweet treats. Almonds are a beloved ingredient in Pugliese desserts, with almond pastries like "pasticciotto" and "cartellate" taking center stage. Pasticciotto is a pastry filled with a luscious custard cream, while cartellate are deep-fried dough spirals soaked in honey or vincotto (cooked wine reduction).

To complement the flavors of the region, Puglia boasts a robust wine industry. Primitivo and Negroamaro are two popular red wine varieties that thrive in the region's sun-drenched vineyards. They are known for their rich, full-bodied flavors that pair perfectly with the hearty dishes of Pugliese cuisine. Pugliese cuisine is a true reflection of the region's history, geography, and cultural heritage. It invites you to savor the simplicity and authenticity of its flavors, transporting you on a gastronomic journey through the sun-kissed landscapes of Puglia. Whether you're enjoying the fresh seafood by the coast or savoring the rustic dishes of the countryside

Traditional Dishes and Local Specialties

Puglia, located in the southern part of Italy, is known for its rich culinary traditions and delicious local specialties. The region's cuisine reflects its geographic location, surrounded by the sea and blessed with fertile land that yields a variety of fresh ingredients. From hearty pasta dishes to succulent seafood and unique desserts, Puglia offers a diverse range of traditional dishes that are sure to delight any food lover. Let's explore some of the traditional dishes and local specialties that make Puglia a gastronomic paradise.

Orecchiette con le Cime di Rapa: Orecchiette, which translates to "little ears," are small, ear-shaped pasta shells that are synonymous with Puglia. This dish combines orecchiette with cime di rapa, a bitter leafy green similar to broccoli rabe. The pasta is typically handmade and served with a sauce made from garlic, olive oil, and chili flakes. Orecchiette con le Cime di Rapa is a simple yet flavorful dish that represents the essence of Puglian cuisine.

Frisella: Frisella is a traditional Puglian bread made from durum wheat flour. It is baked twice to create a dry and crunchy texture. To enjoy frisella, it is typically soaked in water or drizzled with olive oil to soften it. It is then topped with fresh tomatoes, oregano, salt, and extra virgin olive oil. Frisella is a popular snack or appetizer in Puglia, especially during the hot summer months.

Burrata: Burrata is a luscious and creamy cheese that originated in Puglia. It is made from cow's milk and has a soft outer shell with a rich, creamy center. The outer shell is typically made from mozzarella, while the inside is filled with a mixture of cream and stracciatella, a shredded cheese. Burrata is often served with fresh tomatoes, basil, and a drizzle of olive oil, making it a delightful appetizer or addition to salads.

Focaccia Barese: Focaccia Barese is a Puglian version of the popular Italian flatbread. It is thicker and fluffier than other types of focaccia and is typically topped with cherry tomatoes, olives, and oregano. Focaccia Barese is often enjoyed as a snack or served as an accompaniment to antipasti platters.

Polpo alla Pignata: Polpo alla Pignata, or octopus stew, is a beloved seafood dish in Puglia. Tender octopus is simmered in a fragrant tomato sauce with garlic, parsley, and red wine. The stew is slow-cooked in a clay pot, known as a "pignata," which infuses the dish with unique flavors. Polpo alla Pignata is often served with crusty bread to soak up the flavorful sauce.

Cartellate: Cartellate are traditional Puglian pastries that are typically enjoyed during the holiday season. They are made by rolling out thin strips of dough, which are then twisted and fried until golden and crispy. After frying, the pastries are coated in honey, syrup, or vincotto (cooked grape must) and often garnished with almonds or sprinkles. Cartellate are a sweet treat that showcases the skill and artistry of Puglian bakers.

These are just a few examples of the traditional dishes and local specialties that you can savor in Puglia. The region's cuisine is characterized by simple yet robust flavors that highlight the freshness and quality of its ingredients.

Olive Oil and Wine Tasting

Puglia, located in the southern region of Italy, is renowned for its rich culinary traditions and picturesque landscapes. The region boasts a long history of olive oil and wine production, making it a paradise for food and wine enthusiasts. Let's explore the world of olive oil and wine tasting in Puglia.

Olive Oil Tasting: Puglia is often referred to as the "Olive Oil Capital" of Italy, as it produces a significant portion of the country's olive oil. The region is dotted with olive groves, where centuries-old trees thrive under the Mediterranean sun. The local olive varieties, such as Coratina, Ogliarola, and Leccino, contribute to the distinct flavors and aromas of Puglian olive oil.

To delve into the world of Puglian olive oil, a visit to one of the region's olive mills or masserie (traditional farmhouses) is a must. These establishments offer guided tours where you can witness the olive oil production process, from harvesting the olives to pressing them into oil. The passionate producers will educate you about the different olive varieties, the extraction methods, and the factors that influence the oil's quality.

During an olive oil tasting session, you'll have the opportunity to sample various oils, each with its own characteristics. The experts will guide you through the sensory experience, teaching you how to identify the nuances of flavors, bitterness, and spiciness. Puglian olive oil is renowned for its robust and fruity taste, often exhibiting hints of artichoke, almond, and tomato.

Wine Tasting: Puglia's viticulture has a rich history dating back thousands of years. The region is famous for its red wines, particularly the Primitivo and Negroamaro varietals. These grapes thrive in Puglia's warm and sunny climate, producing wines that are deeply colored, full-bodied, and rich in flavor. Exploring Puglia's wine scene involves visiting its picturesque vineyards and wineries. The region offers a diverse range of wine estates, from family-run businesses to larger, well-established producers. Many wineries provide guided tours where you can learn about the winemaking process, from grape cultivation and harvesting to fermentation and aging.

During a wine tasting experience, you'll have the opportunity to sample a variety of Puglian wines, including Primitivo, Negroamaro, and Salice Salentino. The knowledgeable sommeliers will help you appreciate the unique characteristics of each wine, including their aromas, flavors, and structures. Puglian wines are known for their intense fruitiness, with notes of blackberries, cherries, and spices.

Additionally, Puglia's white wines, such as Fiano, Verdeca, and Malvasia, are gaining recognition for their quality and elegance. These wines offer a refreshing alternative and are well worth exploring during your wine tasting journey in Puglia.

Conclusion: Embarking on an olive oil and wine tasting adventure in Puglia is a sensory delight that allows you to immerse yourself in the region's rich gastronomic heritage. Whether you're savoring the robust flavors of Puglian olive oil or indulging in the velvety red wines, you'll be captivated by the passion and craftsmanship of the local producers. Puglia's olive oil and wine tastings offer a truly authentic experience, allowing you to discover the region's flavors, traditions, and the beautiful union between the land and its bounties

Cooking Classes and Food Experiences

Puglia, located in southern Italy, is renowned for its rich culinary traditions and delectable cuisine. If you're a food enthusiast looking to explore the gastronomic wonders of this region, you're in for a treat. Puglia offers a wide range of cooking classes and food experiences that allow you to immerse yourself in the local flavors and learn from expert chefs. Whether you're a novice in the kitchen or an experienced cook, Puglia has something to offer everyone.

Cooking classes in Puglia provide a unique opportunity to learn traditional recipes and techniques directly from local experts. These classes often take place in charming masserie (traditional farmhouses) or cooking schools, where you'll find well-equipped kitchens and a warm, welcoming atmosphere. Experienced chefs will guide you through the preparation of authentic Puglian dishes, using locally sourced ingredients such as fresh seafood, olive oil, vegetables, and aromatic herbs. One of the highlights of cooking classes in Puglia is the focus on handmade pasta. Orecchiette, a type of ear-shaped pasta, is a regional specialty and a staple of Puglian cuisine. During your class, you'll have the chance to learn the art of making this pasta from scratch, from kneading the dough to shaping each delicate piece. You'll also discover other pasta varieties like cavatelli and strascinati, and how to pair them with flavorful sauces. Seafood lovers will be delighted by the abundance of fish and shellfish in Puglia. In cooking classes dedicated to seafood, you'll learn how to select the freshest catch, clean and prepare it, and create mouthwatering dishes that showcase the natural flavors of the sea. From classic recipes like grilled fish with lemon and olive oil to more elaborate seafood stews, you'll gain invaluable skills and knowledge to recreate these dishes at home. Puglia is famous for its olive oil production, so it comes as no surprise that olive oil tastings and workshops are also popular food experiences in the region. You'll have the chance to visit traditional olive groves, learn about the cultivation and harvesting process, and understand the different varieties and qualities of olive oil. Expert tasters will guide you through a sensory journey, teaching you how to recognize the nuances of flavor, aroma, and texture in olive oils. Beyond cooking classes, Puglia offers a range of immersive food experiences that allow you to discover the region's culinary heritage. Food tours take you through bustling local markets, where you can interact with vendors, sample fresh produce, and learn about the ingredients that form the basis of Puglian cuisine. You can also visit family-run farms and wineries, where you'll witness the production of cheese, wine, and other traditional products firsthand. Puglia's food experiences extend beyond the kitchen and the table. You can participate in countryside foraging excursions, guided by experts who will teach you how to identify and collect wild herbs, mushrooms, and edible plants that are used in local recipes. These outings provide a deeper connection to the region's natural resources and offer a glimpse into the traditional ways of gathering ingredients.

In conclusion, Puglia is a food lover's paradise, offering a plethora of cooking classes and food experiences that showcase the region's culinary treasures. Whether you're interested in mastering pasta-making, exploring seafood delights, or delving into olive oil appreciation, Puglia has something to satisfy every palate. Embark on a gastronomic journey through Puglia and indulge in the flavors and traditions that make this region a true culinary gem

Puglia's Food Festivals

Puglia, a charming region located in southern Italy, is not only known for its stunning landscapes and rich cultural heritage but also for its vibrant food scene. Throughout the year, Puglia hosts numerous food festivals that showcase the region's culinary delights and traditional dishes. These festivals are a celebration of local ingredients, flavors, and gastronomic traditions, attracting both locals and tourists alike. Let's explore some of the notable food festivals in Puglia.

Festa della Taranta: While not strictly a food festival, Festa della Taranta is a highly anticipated annual event held in Salento, Puglia. It celebrates the region's rich musical and cultural heritage, with traditional folk music and dance performances taking center stage. Alongside the music, visitors can indulge in a variety of local culinary treats, including street food specialties like puccia (a type of sandwich) and frisella (a type of dry bread topped with fresh ingredients).

Sagra della Bruschetta: Held in the town of Carovigno, this festival is a paradise for bruschetta lovers. Bruschetta, a popular Italian antipasto made with grilled bread topped with various toppings, takes the spotlight here. Visitors can savor a wide range of bruschetta variations, from simple classics like tomato and basil to creative combinations featuring local ingredients such as fresh seafood, wild mushrooms, and local cheeses. It's a delightful event that showcases the region's culinary creativity.

Festa del Pane e dell'Olio: This festival, dedicated to bread and olive oil, is celebrated in the town of Altamura. Altamura is renowned for its traditional bread, Pane di Altamura, which is made from a specific type of wheat called "Senatore Cappelli." During the festival, visitors can witness the traditional bread-making process and taste various bread varieties. Additionally, local olive oil producers showcase their products, offering the opportunity to sample different olive oils and learn about the olive oil production techniques.

Fiera del Peperone di Senise: Although technically located in the neighboring region of Basilicata, the Fiera del Peperone di Senise is worth mentioning as it attracts many visitors from Puglia. This festival celebrates the famous Senise pepper, a spicy red pepper with a rich flavor. Visitors can enjoy a wide array of dishes prepared with this unique ingredient, including traditional pasta dishes, spicy sauces, and preserved peppers. The festival also features cultural events, live music, and exhibitions.

La Festa del Mare: As a coastal region, Puglia boasts an abundance of fresh seafood, and the Festa del Mare (Festival of the Sea) celebrates this coastal bounty. The festival takes place in numerous coastal towns, such as Gallipoli, Monopoli, and Trani, where visitors can indulge in a wide range of seafood delicacies, including raw and cooked fish, shellfish, and traditional fish-based dishes like tiella and brodetto. The festival often includes lively music performances, exhibitions, and cooking demonstrations.

These are just a few examples of the many food festivals that Puglia has to offer. Whether you're a food enthusiast or simply looking to immerse yourself in the region's vibrant culinary culture, attending these festivals provides a fantastic opportunity to experience the authentic flavors of Puglia and create unforgettable memories

Best Restaurants and Local Eateries

Puglia, located in the southern region of Italy, is known for its stunning coastline, picturesque towns, and rich culinary traditions. The region boasts a vibrant food scene that celebrates the freshest local ingredients and traditional recipes. From fresh seafood to handmade pasta and flavorful olive oil, Puglia offers a diverse range of dishes that are sure to delight any food lover. Here are some of the best restaurants and local eateries in Puglia.

Osteria del Tempo Perso (Ostuni): Situated in the charming town of Ostuni, Osteria del Tempo Perso is a must-visit for those seeking authentic Puglian cuisine. The restaurant focuses on traditional recipes with a modern twist, using locally sourced ingredients. From their delicious homemade pasta dishes to the mouthwatering seafood specialties, every bite at Osteria del Tempo Perso is a true delight.

Antichi Sapori (Montegrosso di Andria): Located in the heart of the Puglian countryside, Antichi Sapori is a rustic farmhouse restaurant that serves some of the best traditional dishes in the region. The menu features an array of local delicacies, including orecchiette (ear-shaped pasta), lamb, and a variety of seasonal vegetables.

Al Fornello da Ricci (Cisternino): Nestled in the historic town of Cisternino, Al Fornello da Ricci is a family-run trattoria renowned for its meat dishes, particularly the succulent grilled meats and sausages. The restaurant's cozy ambiance and friendly staff make it a favorite among locals and visitors alike. Be sure to try their famous bombette, which are delicious, cheese-stuffed meat rolls.

Masseria Il Frantoio (Ostuni): For a unique and unforgettable dining experience, head to Masseria Il Frantoio. This beautiful masseria (traditional farmhouse) offers a farm-to-table concept, serving dishes made with ingredients grown on-site. The menu showcases traditional Puglian flavors and includes homemade pasta, fresh vegetables, and aromatic olive oil produced from their own olive groves.

Ristorante Grotta Palazzese (Polignano a Mare): Set in a stunning location inside a limestone cave overlooking the Adriatic Sea, Ristorante Grotta Palazzese offers a dining experience like no other. The cave's natural beauty combined with the restaurant's gourmet cuisine creates a magical atmosphere. Enjoy fresh seafood and traditional Puglian dishes while taking in the breathtaking views.

Cibus (Bari): Located in the lively city of Bari, Cibus is a contemporary restaurant that offers a creative twist on Puglian cuisine. The menu features innovative dishes prepared with locally sourced ingredients, highlighting the region's culinary heritage in a modern way. The stylish ambiance and attentive service make Cibus a popular choice among food enthusiasts.

La Locanda di Nonna Mena (Ceglie Messapica): Tucked away in the charming town of Ceglie Messapica, La Locanda di Nonna Mena is a family-run trattoria known for its authentic and hearty Puglian dishes. The menu showcases the traditional flavors of the region, with dishes like frisella (a local bread specialty), vegetable soups, and slow-cooked meats. The warm hospitality and cozy atmosphere make it a true gem.

These are just a few examples of the best restaurants and local eateries in Puglia. The region is filled with culinary treasures waiting to be discovered, and exploring the local cuisine is a delightful journey for your taste buds.

Puglia's Natural Wonders and Outdoor Activities

Gargano Peninsula: Nature's Playground

The Gargano Peninsula, located in the picturesque region of Puglia, Italy, is a captivating destination known as "Nature's Playground." With its diverse landscapes, rich biodiversity, and stunning coastal beauty, the Gargano Peninsula offers a unique and unforgettable experience for nature lovers and adventure seekers alike.

Stretching out into the Adriatic Sea, the Gargano Peninsula is characterized by its dramatic cliffs, secluded coves, and pristine beaches. The coastline is a true paradise, with crystal-clear turquoise waters inviting visitors to swim, snorkel, and explore underwater marvels. One of the most famous beach destinations is Vieste, a charming town boasting golden sands and impressive sea stacks rising majestically from the water.

Beyond its stunning beaches, the Gargano Peninsula is a haven for outdoor enthusiasts. The peninsula is home to the Gargano National Park, a protected area encompassing over 120,000 acres of natural wonders. Within the park, visitors can explore dense forests, lush meadows, and picturesque lakes. The Umbra Forest, with its ancient beech trees and winding trails, offers a peaceful retreat for hikers and nature lovers. The park is also home to Monte Sant'Angelo, a UNESCO World Heritage Site known for its historic architecture and breathtaking views of the surrounding landscape.

For those seeking adventure, the Gargano Peninsula offers a range of exciting activities. The rugged terrain is ideal for hiking, mountain biking, and horseback riding, allowing visitors to immerse themselves in the region's natural beauty. Thrill-seekers can also embark on a thrilling rock climbing expedition, scaling the cliffs that line the coastline for an adrenaline-pumping experience.

One of the most iconic landmarks of the Gargano Peninsula is the Tremiti Islands, a small archipelago consisting of five stunning islands. These islands are a true gem of the Adriatic, with their secluded beaches, transparent waters, and fascinating marine life. Visitors can take a boat tour to explore the islands, dive into the vibrant underwater world, or simply relax and soak up the tranquility of these hidden paradises.

The Gargano Peninsula is not only a sanctuary for natural beauty but also boasts a rich cultural heritage. The towns and villages scattered throughout the region offer a glimpse into the authentic Italian way of life. From the charming streets of Peschici to the historic charm of Rodi Garganico, each town has its own unique character and traditions. Visitors can indulge in local cuisine, sample regional wines, and experience the warmth and hospitality of the local people.

In conclusion, the Gargano Peninsula is a nature lover's dream and a true playground for those seeking outdoor adventure. With its breathtaking landscapes, stunning beaches, and diverse wildlife, this region of Puglia offers a unique and unforgettable experience. Whether you're hiking through ancient forests, diving into azure waters, or simply taking in the beauty of the coastline, the Gargano Peninsula will captivate your heart and leave you with lasting memories of its natural splendor

Valle d'Itria: Rolling Hills and Countryside:

Valle d'Itria, located in the southern Italian region of Puglia, is a breathtaking area known for its rolling hills, picturesque countryside, and unique architectural heritage. This enchanting valley stretches across the provinces of Bari, Brindisi, and Taranto, offering visitors a glimpse into the authentic beauty of rural Italy. One of the defining features of Valle d'Itria is its distinctive landscape, characterized by gently sloping hills covered in lush greenery. Olive groves, vineyards, and fields of wheat and sunflowers dot the countryside, creating a tapestry of vibrant colors that change with the seasons. The idyllic scenery is often compared to a painting, captivating the hearts of all who visit. What sets Valle d'Itria apart from other regions in Italy is its iconic trulli houses. These unique stone dwellings with cone-shaped roofs are a testament to the area's rich history and traditional architecture. Dating back centuries, trulli were originally built as temporary shelters for agricultural workers but have since become a symbol of the region. The town of Alberobello, a UNESCO World Heritage site, is renowned for its dense concentration of trulli, forming a fairytale-like village that attracts countless tourists each year. Beyond the trulli, Valle d'Itria boasts a string of charming towns and villages waiting to be explored. Locorotondo, a hilltop town known for its circular layout and whitewashed houses, offers panoramic views of the surrounding countryside. Ostuni, often referred to as the "White City," features a maze of narrow streets, dazzling white buildings, and a stunning medieval cathedral. Cisternino and Martina Franca, with their historic centers and lively atmospheres, are also worth a visit. Apart from its architectural marvels, Valle d'Itria is a gastronomic paradise. The region is renowned for its olive oil production, and you'll find countless olive groves and oil mills offering tastings and tours. Puglia's culinary delights, including handmade pasta, fresh seafood, and local wines, can be savored in the rustic trattorias and family-run restaurants scattered throughout the valley. Don't miss the opportunity to try the famous orecchiette, a traditional pasta shape that resembles little ears. For those seeking outdoor adventures, Valle d'Itria offers ample opportunities for exploration. You can embark on hiking or cycling excursions through the picturesque countryside, taking in the beauty of the rolling hills and vineyards. The region is also dotted with charming agriturismi, where you can stay on working farms and experience the rural way of life firsthand.

Valle d'Itria is a place that captures the essence of rural Italy, with its stunning landscapes, unique architecture, rich history, and warm hospitality. Whether you're strolling through the narrow streets of Alberobello, enjoying a meal of fresh local produce, or simply admiring the panoramic views, this enchanting valley will leave an indelible mark on your heart and soul.

Salento Peninsula: Sun, Sea, and Sand:

The Salento Peninsula, located in the southernmost region of Italy known as Puglia, is a captivating destination that offers an idyllic combination of sun, sea, and sand. With its stunning coastline, crystal-clear waters, and charming towns, Salento has become a beloved hotspot for travelers seeking a quintessential Mediterranean experience. One of the main draws of the Salento Peninsula is its remarkable beaches. The region boasts a diverse array of coastal landscapes, ranging from long stretches of golden sand to hidden coves nestled between rugged cliffs. Whether you prefer lively and bustling beach resorts or secluded and untouched paradises, Salento has something for everyone. Some of the most renowned beaches include Punta Prosciutto, Porto Cesareo, Torre dell'Orso, and Baia dei Turchi. These pristine shores provide ample opportunities for swimming, sunbathing, water sports, or simply relaxing while soaking up the Mediterranean sun. Aside from its enchanting beaches, Salento is known for its crystalline turquoise waters. The sea here is exceptionally clear and inviting, making it perfect for snorkeling and diving enthusiasts. Exploring the underwater world reveals a stunning array of marine life and colorful coral reefs, offering unforgettable experiences for nature lovers.

While the natural beauty of the Salento Peninsula is undoubtedly its main allure, the region also boasts a rich cultural heritage. The historic towns and cities in Salento are adorned with Baroque architecture, ancient ruins, and charming narrow streets. Lecce, often referred to as the "Florence of the South," is renowned for its magnificent Baroque buildings, including the Basilica di Santa Croce and the Piazza del Duomo. Otranto, with its impressive Aragonese Castle and charming old town, is another must-visit destination. Salento's culinary scene is also a highlight, showcasing the region's gastronomic traditions. Puglian cuisine is known for its simple yet flavorful dishes, featuring fresh seafood, locally produced olive oil, and an abundance of vegetables. Don't miss the opportunity to savor traditional delicacies such as orecchiette pasta, burrata cheese, friselle (dried bread), and pasticciotto (a sweet pastry).

Furthermore, Salento is renowned for its vibrant and lively festivals, where locals and visitors come together to celebrate the region's cultural heritage. The Taranta Festival, dedicated to the traditional dance known as "pizzica," takes place throughout the summer, featuring music, dancing, and folklore performances. It is a true feast for the senses, immersing you in the lively spirit of Salento.

Whether you seek relaxation on pristine beaches, exploration of historic sites, culinary delights, or cultural immersion, the Salento Peninsula offers a remarkable holiday experience. With its captivating blend of sun, sea, sand, and authentic Italian charm, Salento has rightfully earned its place as a beloved destination in Puglia.

Tremiti Islands: Pristine Marine Life:

The Tremiti Islands, located off the coast of Puglia in southern Italy, are a hidden gem renowned for their pristine marine life. Composed of five main islands - San Domino, San Nicola, Capraia, Cretaccio, and Pianosa - this archipelago offers an unparalleled experience for nature enthusiasts and diving aficionados. One of the most captivating aspects of the Tremiti Islands is their crystal-clear turquoise waters, which teem with a rich diversity of marine species. Thanks to the area's protected status as a marine reserve, the ecosystem has flourished undisturbed, resulting in an abundance of underwater life. Diving and snorkeling enthusiasts are treated to a kaleidoscope of colors and shapes as they explore the depths of the surrounding sea. Vibrant coral reefs, submerged caves, and dramatic rock formations create a mesmerizing underwater landscape. These natural habitats provide shelter and nourishment for an array of species, including colorful fish, octopuses, sea turtles, and even dolphins.

One of the standout features of the Tremiti Islands is the opportunity to witness the Posidonia oceanica meadows. Posidonia oceanica, a seagrass endemic to the Mediterranean, plays a crucial role in maintaining the health of the marine ecosystem. These underwater meadows act as nurseries for numerous species, provide oxygen, and contribute to the water's exceptional clarity. Exploring the Posidonia meadows is like entering a secret garden, where the delicate seagrass sways in harmony with the tides. For those who prefer to stay dry but still want to experience the wonders of the sea, boat excursions are an excellent option. The islands' unique geography features rugged cliffs and secluded coves, which are best explored by sea. Boat tours allow visitors to discover hidden caves, grottoes, and secluded beaches, all while taking in the awe-inspiring beauty of the surrounding marine environment. Above the waterline, the Tremiti Islands are equally captivating. The islands boast a rugged coastline, characterized by towering cliffs and dramatic vistas. San Domino, the largest and most inhabited island, is renowned for its sandy beaches and crystal-clear waters. Visitors can relax on the pristine shores, basking in the Mediterranean sun, or explore the island's interior, which is dotted with fragrant pine forests and walking trails.

San Nicola, the second-largest island, is dominated by a picturesque medieval fortress. The island's charming village offers a glimpse into the region's rich history and provides breathtaking views of the surrounding sea. Capraia, Cretaccio, and Pianosa, though smaller and uninhabited, offer visitors a sense of solitude and tranquility amidst their unspoiled natural landscapes.

Whether you're an avid diver, nature enthusiast, or simply seeking a peaceful retreat surrounded by pristine beauty, the Tremiti Islands are a must-visit destination. With their abundant marine life, stunning landscapes, and secluded beaches, these islands offer a truly unforgettable experience in the heart of the Mediterranean

Hiking and Cycling Routes

Puglia, located in southern Italy, is a breathtaking region known for its beautiful landscapes, charming towns, and stunning coastline. It offers a diverse range of outdoor activities, including hiking and cycling, making it an ideal destination for nature enthusiasts. Whether you prefer exploring coastal trails or venturing through picturesque countryside, Puglia has something to offer for everyone. Here are some popular hiking and cycling routes in Puglia:

Gargano Promontory: The Gargano Promontory, also known as the "spur of Italy," offers a variety of hiking trails with magnificent views of the Adriatic Sea. One of the most famous routes is the "Gargano Promontory Coastal Path," which stretches for about 60 kilometers from Vieste to Mattinata. Along the way, you'll encounter rugged cliffs, hidden coves, and picturesque fishing villages.

Salento Peninsula: The Salento Peninsula, located in the southernmost part of Puglia, is a paradise for both hikers and cyclists. The "Salento Ring" is a popular cycling route that takes you through olive groves, vineyards, and charming villages. For hikers, the "Sentiero del Ciolo" offers a scenic coastal trail that winds along dramatic cliffs, providing breathtaking views of the turquoise waters below.

Alberobello and the Itria Valley: Alberobello, a UNESCO World Heritage site famous for its unique cone-shaped houses called trulli, is a great starting point for exploring the beautiful Itria Valley. You can hike or cycle through the valley's rolling hills, dotted with vineyards and olive groves, and visit picturesque towns like Locorotondo and Cisternino along the way.

Murgia National Park: Located near the city of Matera, in the neighboring region of Basilicata, Murgia National Park offers a stunning natural landscape for outdoor enthusiasts. The park features ancient cave dwellings, rocky plateaus, and deep ravines. Hiking and mountain biking trails crisscross the park, providing opportunities to explore its unique flora and fauna.

Coastal Trails in Puglia: Puglia boasts a beautiful coastline with crystal-clear waters and stunning cliffs. Along the coast, you'll find several scenic trails that are perfect for hiking and cycling. The "Baia dei Turchi" near Otranto is a popular spot for coastal hikes, while the "Cycling Path of the Two Seas" connects the Adriatic and Ionian coasts, allowing cyclists to enjoy breathtaking views throughout their journey. When exploring hiking and cycling routes in Puglia, it's important to plan accordingly, especially considering weather conditions and the difficulty level of the trails. It's also recommended to bring proper gear, carry sufficient water and snacks, and adhere to any safety guidelines provided by local authorities or park rangers. Whether you choose to hike along the stunning coastlines, pedal through picturesque countryside, or explore historic towns and villages,

Puglia offers a wealth of natural beauty and outdoor adventure for hikers and cyclists alike

Water Sports and Beach Activities

Puglia, located in southern Italy, is known for its breathtaking coastline along the Adriatic and Ionian Seas. With its crystal-clear waters, sandy beaches, and pleasant climate, Puglia offers a wide range of water sports and beach activities for visitors to enjoy. Whether you're seeking adventure, relaxation, or simply a fun-filled day by the sea, Puglia has something to offer for everyone. Here are some popular water sports and beach activities you can enjoy in Puglia:

Swimming and Sunbathing: Puglia boasts numerous beautiful beaches where you can relax, soak up the sun, and take refreshing dips in the sparkling waters. From the golden sands of Polignano a Mare to the pristine shores of Porto Cesareo, there are plenty of idyllic spots to enjoy a leisurely beach day.

Snorkeling and Diving: The coastal waters of Puglia are rich in marine life and offer excellent snorkeling and diving opportunities. Explore the vibrant underwater world, discover colorful coral reefs, and encounter various species of fish and other marine creatures. The Tremiti Islands and the protected marine area of Porto Cesareo are particularly popular for snorkeling and diving excursions.

Kayaking and Stand-Up Paddleboarding: Embark on a kayaking or stand-up paddleboarding adventure along the coast of Puglia. Navigate through sea caves, explore hidden coves, and enjoy breathtaking views of cliffs and rock formations. Many coastal towns in Puglia offer rentals and guided tours for these activities.

Windsurfing and Kitesurfing: Puglia's windy conditions make it an ideal destination for windsurfing and kitesurfing enthusiasts. The region's long stretches of coastline provide ample space and favorable wind conditions for thrilling rides and jumps. Some popular spots for these activities include Porto Cesareo, Punta Prosciutto, and the Gargano Peninsula.

Sailing and Boat Trips: Charter a sailboat or join a boat tour to discover the stunning coastal landscapes of Puglia. Sail along the Adriatic coast, visit charming fishing villages, and anchor in secluded bays. Boat trips often include stops for swimming, snorkeling, and enjoying delicious local cuisine.

Jet Skiing and Water Skiing: For those seeking adrenaline-pumping water sports, jet skiing and water skiing are popular options in Puglia. Experience the thrill of speeding across the water and enjoy the beautiful coastal scenery from a different perspective. Many beach resorts and water sports centers provide rentals and lessons for these activities.

Fishing and Boat Excursions: Puglia's fishing traditions are deeply rooted in its coastal communities. Join a fishing excursion to experience traditional fishing techniques and learn from local fishermen. Alternatively, you can also hire a boat for a leisurely day of fishing in the Mediterranean waters.

Beach Volleyball and Beach Soccer: Puglia's sandy beaches offer the perfect setting for beach sports such as volleyball and soccer. Gather a group of friends or join a local team for a friendly match on the beach. Many beach clubs and resorts provide designated areas for these activities. Remember to check local regulations, weather conditions, and safety guidelines before participating in any water sports or beach activities. Whether you're seeking adventure or relaxation, Puglia's stunning coastline and azure waters provide a wonderful backdrop for a memorable water-filled vacation

Puglia's Festivals and Events

6.1 Carnival celebrations: in Puglia, Italy, are vibrant and colorful events that bring communities together in a festive atmosphere. Puglia, located in the southern part of Italy, has a rich cultural heritage, and its Carnival traditions reflect this diversity and uniqueness. Carnival in Puglia is a time of joy and merriment, with locals and visitors alike donning elaborate costumes, masks, and accessories. The festivities typically begin in January and culminate on Shrove Tuesday, also known as Fat Tuesday or Martedì Grasso, which is the day before Ash Wednesday and the start of Lent. One of the most renowned Carnival celebrations in Puglia takes place in the town of Putignano. Dating back over 600 years, the Putignano Carnival is the oldest in Italy and attracts thousands of spectators each year. The highlight of the Putignano Carnival is the parade of allegorical floats adorned with intricate decorations and accompanied by costumed performers. The floats often depict satirical representations of current events and famous personalities, creating a playful and humorous atmosphere. Another notable Carnival celebration in Puglia occurs in the town of Galatina. Known as the "Taranta Carnival," it combines the traditions of Carnival with the region's famous folk dance, the "Pizzica Tarantata." During this celebration, the streets come alive with music, dance, and traditional costumes, as locals and visitors participate in lively processions and performances. The Taranta Carnival is a unique fusion of Carnival revelry and the vibrant music and dance culture of Puglia. In addition to Putignano and Galatina, many other towns and cities throughout Puglia also hold their own Carnival celebrations. From Lecce to Bari, Brindisi to Trani, each place adds its own flavor and customs to the festivities. These celebrations often include costume contests, masquerade balls, street performances, and delicious food and drink. Food plays a significant role in Carnival celebrations in Puglia. Traditional Carnival treats include "frappe" or "chiacchiere" (fried sweet dough sprinkled with powdered sugar), "castagnole" (small round pastries), and "cartellate" (deep-fried dough strips coated in honey). These delectable treats are enjoyed by both young and old during the Carnival season. Carnival in Puglia is not only a time for revelry but also a celebration of community and tradition. It brings people together to create lasting memories and strengthen social bonds. Whether it's the elaborate parades, the lively music and dance, or the delicious food, Carnival in Puglia offers a unique and unforgettable experience for all who participate. So, if you find yourself in Puglia during Carnival season, make sure to join in the festivities, immerse yourself in the vibrant atmosphere, and discover the rich cultural heritage that makes Carnival in Puglia a truly special event

Holy Week Processions

Holy Week processions in Puglia, Italy, are vibrant and deeply rooted in the region's rich religious and cultural traditions. Puglia, located in the southeastern part of the country, is known for its devout Catholic population, and during Holy Week, the streets come alive with elaborate processions that depict the Passion of Christ. One of the most significant Holy Week processions in Puglia takes place in Taranto, a coastal city with a strong religious heritage. The Processione dei Misteri di Taranto (Procession of the Mysteries of Taranto) is a grand event that attracts thousands of locals and visitors each year. The procession is held on Good Friday and involves the procession of statues depicting scenes from the Passion, carried by the members of various religious brotherhoods. These statues, known as "Misteri," are beautifully crafted and depict different moments of Christ's Passion, such as the Last Supper, the Crucifixion, and the Descent from the Cross. The statues are adorned with rich fabrics, flowers, and candles, creating a solemn and awe-inspiring atmosphere. The procession winds its way through the streets of Taranto, accompanied by prayers, hymns, and the mournful sound of the "Misteri" being carried on the shoulders of the devotees.

Another noteworthy Holy Week procession in Puglia takes place in Molfetta, a charming coastal town. The Processione della Sacra Spina (Procession of the Holy Thorn) is a unique event that occurs on Holy Thursday. The highlight of this procession is a reliquary containing a thorn, believed to be from Christ's Crown of Thorns. The reliquary is paraded through the streets, followed by a solemn procession of religious brotherhoods and the local clergy. The streets of Molfetta are adorned with religious decorations and lit up by countless candles, creating an ethereal ambiance. The procession stops at several designated stations, where prayers are recited and hymns are sung. The people of Molfetta deeply engage with this event, participating in prayers and reflections as they accompany the relic through the town.

In addition to Taranto and Molfetta, many other towns and cities in Puglia hold Holy Week processions that showcase their local traditions and faith. Each procession is unique, featuring its distinct rituals, statues, and devotional practices. Locals and tourists alike gather to witness these events, paying homage to the religious significance of Holy Week and experiencing the profound devotion of the Pugliese people. These processions not only serve as religious ceremonies but also serve as a cultural expression and a way to connect the present with centuries of tradition. The passion, artistry, and devotion displayed during the Holy Week processions in Puglia create an unforgettable experience, leaving a lasting impression on all who witness them.

Folklore and Traditional Festivals

Puglia, located in southern Italy, is a region rich in folklore and traditional festivals that reflect its cultural heritage and historical significance. These festivities celebrate the region's religious beliefs, agricultural traditions, and local customs. Let's explore some of the prominent folklore and traditional festivals in Puglia.

Taranta Festival: One of the most famous festivals in Puglia is the Taranta Festival, also known as the Notte della Taranta. This event is a celebration of traditional music and dance, particularly the Pizzica, a folk dance associated with the tarantula spider bite cure. During the festival, which takes place in various towns across the region, musicians and dancers come together to perform and preserve this ancient tradition.

Procession of the Mysteries: Held in the city of Taranto during Holy Week, the Procession of the Mysteries (Processione dei Misteri) is a solemn and religious event. Participants carry large wooden statues representing scenes from the Passion of Christ through the streets of the city. The procession is accompanied by liturgical music and chants, creating a somber atmosphere.

Cavalcata di Sant'Oronzo: This festival honors the patron saint of the city of Lecce, Sant'Oronzo. It takes place on August 25th and is a vibrant and colorful event. The festival features a grand parade with horses and floats adorned with flowers and traditional costumes. The highlight is the statue of Sant'Oronzo, carried through the streets, while people celebrate with music, dancing, and fireworks.

Festival della Taranta: Similar to the Taranta Festival mentioned earlier, the Festival della Taranta is held in Melpignano, a town in the province of Lecce. It is a week-long celebration of Pizzica music and dance, attracting both locals and tourists. The festival culminates in a grand concert where renowned musicians perform alongside local artists, creating an unforgettable experience.

Festa di Sant'Agata: Celebrated in the city of Gallipoli, the Festa di Sant'Agata honors Saint Agatha, the patron saint of the city. The festival takes place on February 4th and 5th and includes religious processions, fireworks, and traditional culinary specialties. It is a significant event for the local community, with devotees participating in the procession and expressing their devotion to the saint.

Fiera di San Giorgio: The Fiera di San Giorgio is an ancient fair held in the town of Apricena, dedicated to Saint George, the patron saint of the region. It takes place on the last Sunday of April and features a lively market where local artisans showcase their products, including traditional ceramics, textiles, and food. The fair also includes exhibitions, musical performances, and equestrian shows. These are just a few examples of the folklore and traditional festivals that take place in Puglia. Each event represents a unique aspect of the region's history, cultural heritage, and religious beliefs. Attending these festivals offers a wonderful opportunity to immerse oneself in the vibrant traditions and customs of Puglia, creating unforgettable memories.

Music and Cultural Events

Puglia, a captivating region in southern Italy, not only boasts stunning landscapes and delectable cuisine but also hosts a vibrant music and cultural scene. From traditional folk music to modern music festivals, Puglia offers a diverse range of musical and cultural events that attract both locals and tourists alike. Let's delve into some of the highlights of music and cultural events in Puglia.

Taranta festival: Puglia is renowned for its rich folk music heritage, and the Taranta Festival is a celebration of the region's traditional music and dance. Held in the town of Melpignano, this festival takes place in August and features performances by renowned musicians, including tarantella orchestras and international artists. The festival culminates in a mesmerizing outdoor concert where thousands of people gather to dance the traditional Pizzica dance.

Locus Festival: For music enthusiasts seeking a blend of contemporary sounds and historic venues, the Locus Festival is a must-visit. Held in various locations across Puglia, including the enchanting city of Locorotondo, this festival showcases a diverse range of musical genres, such as jazz, rock, blues, and world music. The performances take place in unique settings, such as historic churches and courtyards, adding an extra touch of charm to the overall experience.

La Notte della Taranta: This annual music festival is one of the most significant cultural events in Puglia. It spans several weeks during the summer, with various concerts and workshops held in different towns throughout the region. La Notte della Taranta culminates in a grand finale concert in the town of Melpignano, where acclaimed artists come together to perform captivating renditions of traditional folk songs, captivating audiences with their lively rhythms and heartfelt melodies.

Festival della Valle d'Itria: For lovers of classical music and opera, the Festival della Valle d'Itria is a highlight on Puglia's cultural calendar. Held in the picturesque town of Martina Franca, this festival showcases a repertoire of operatic performances, chamber music concerts, and ballet productions. The enchanting atmosphere of the historic town, coupled with the outstanding performances, makes this festival an unforgettable experience for music aficionados.

Puglia Sounds: Puglia Sounds is an initiative aimed at promoting and supporting the region's contemporary music scene. It organizes a series of events throughout the year, including concerts, showcases, and music conferences, highlighting emerging local talents as well as attracting renowned national and international artists. Puglia Sounds also offers support and resources for musicians and music industry professionals, contributing to the growth and development of the local music scene. Apart from these major events, Puglia also hosts numerous smaller-scale festivals, cultural exhibitions, and street performances throughout the year. The region's vibrant music and cultural scene reflect the deep-rooted traditions and diverse influences that have shaped Puglia's identity. Whether you're a music lover or a culture enthusiast, exploring the music and cultural events in Puglia is an excellent way to immerse yourself in the region's rich heritage and experience the magic of southern Italy.

Wine and Food Festivals

Puglia, located in the southern region of Italy, is renowned for its exquisite wines, rich culinary traditions, and vibrant food festivals. With its favorable climate, fertile soil, and proximity to the Mediterranean Sea, Puglia has become a haven for wine and food enthusiasts. Let's explore some of the remarkable wine and food festivals that take place in this enchanting region.

Cantine Aperte: Held annually in May, Cantine Aperte (Open Cellars) is a nationwide event that celebrates the wine culture of Italy. Many wineries in Puglia participate in this event, opening their doors to visitors who can enjoy guided tours, wine tastings, and learn about the winemaking process firsthand. It's an excellent opportunity to sample a wide variety of local wines while exploring the stunning vineyards of Puglia.

Vinòforum: Vinòforum is a prominent wine festival that takes place in Brindisi, a city known for its wine production. Held in June, this event brings together wine lovers, industry professionals, and wine producers from across Italy. Visitors can attend tastings, seminars, and workshops led by renowned sommeliers and winemakers. It's a fantastic opportunity to discover the diverse range of wines produced in Puglia and learn about the local winemaking traditions.

La Festa della Taranta: Although not solely focused on wine and food, La Festa della Taranta is an iconic music and cultural festival that takes place in various towns throughout Salento, a subregion of Puglia. This vibrant festival celebrates the traditional dance known as "pizzica" and features numerous live performances by local musicians. During the festivities, visitors can enjoy street food stalls serving a variety of delicious regional dishes and sample local wines while immersing themselves in the lively atmosphere.

Gusto Dopa Teglia: Located in the town of Andria, Gusto Dopa Teglia is a gastronomic festival dedicated to a typical local dish called "Gusto Dopa Teglia." This dish consists of a generous portion of focaccia topped with tomatoes, onions, olives, and a variety of other ingredients. The festival typically takes place in August, attracting numerous food enthusiasts who can indulge in this mouthwatering specialty and savor the local flavors of Andria.

Sagra della Bruschetta: The town of Carovigno hosts the Sagra della Bruschetta, a festival that celebrates the humble yet delicious bruschetta. Held in July, this festival showcases various creative toppings on toasted bread, including fresh tomatoes, olive oil, local cheeses, cured meats, and more. Visitors can stroll through the charming streets, sampling different bruschetta varieties and enjoying the lively atmosphere filled with music and entertainment.

Olive Oil Festivals: Puglia is renowned for its high-quality olive oil production, and several towns in the region host olive oil festivals to celebrate this culinary treasure. In November, the town of Fasano organizes the Sagra della Olive, where visitors can taste different olive oils, learn about the olive pressing process, and explore the local culinary traditions associated with this precious ingredient. Similarly, the town of Carpino holds the Festa dell'Olio Novello, dedicated to the new harvest of olive oil, featuring tastings, food stalls, and cultural events. These are just a few examples of the wine and food festivals that take place in Puglia. With its rich culinary heritage, stunning landscapes, and warm hospitality, Puglia offers a remarkable experience for those seeking to indulge in the region's extraordinary wines and flavorsome cuisine.

Puglia's Summer Festivities

Puglia, located in the southern region of Italy, is renowned for its breathtaking landscapes, stunning coastline, and rich cultural heritage. During the summer season, Puglia truly comes alive with a vibrant array of festivities that showcase the region's traditions, cuisine, music, and warm hospitality. Let's dive into some of the captivating summer festivities in Puglia.

La Notte della Taranta: La Notte della Taranta is a world-famous music festival celebrated throughout the Salento peninsula in Puglia. This festival pays homage to the traditional dance form known as "pizzica," which is deeply rooted in the region's history. During the event, various towns and villages host concerts and performances by renowned musicians and dancers, creating an enchanting atmosphere where locals and visitors alike can immerse themselves in the exhilarating rhythms of Puglian folk music.

Feast of Saint Oronzo: In August, the city of Lecce honors its patron saint, Saint Oronzo, with a grand celebration. The Feast of Saint Oronzo, known as "La Festa di San'Oronzo," combines religious processions, lively parades, stunning fireworks, and traditional performances. The streets are adorned with colorful decorations, and locals participate in festivities that showcase the city's unique Baroque architecture, traditional costumes, and local delicacies.

The Night of the Myth: In the town of Grottaglie, renowned for its ancient pottery traditions, The Night of the Myth takes place during the summer months. This event is a fascinating blend of history, art, and folklore. The streets come alive with street performers, artists, and craftsmen showcasing their skills. The night culminates with a magnificent parade featuring mythical creatures, giant puppets, and elaborate floats, evoking a sense of wonder and enchantment.

Fish Festivals: Being a coastal region, Puglia celebrates its strong connection with the sea through numerous fish festivals that take place in various towns along the Adriatic and Ionian coastlines. These festivals highlight the bounty of the sea and the traditional fishing heritage of Puglia. Visitors can savor a variety of freshly caught seafood, including octopus, mussels, anchovies, and other local delicacies, while enjoying live music, dancing, and a convivial atmosphere.

Wine Festivals: Puglia is also known for its excellent wines, and several wine festivals occur during the summer season. These festivals celebrate the region's viticulture and offer the opportunity to taste a wide range of local wines, including the famous Primitivo and Negroamaro varieties. Visitors can attend wine tastings, vineyard tours, and learn about the winemaking process while enjoying traditional food pairings and live entertainment.

Summer Concerts and Theater: Throughout the summer months, Puglia hosts a series of outdoor concerts and theater performances, attracting both local and international artists. From classical music to contemporary performances, these events take place in historical venues, picturesque squares, and enchanting landscapes, offering a unique cultural experience against the backdrop of Puglia's natural beauty. These are just a few examples of the summer festivities that take place in Puglia. Each celebration showcases the region's distinct traditions, culinary delights, and vibrant spirit, providing a memorable experience for visitors who want to immerse themselves in the captivating culture of this beautiful Italian region

Puglia's Hidden Gems and Off-the-Beaten-Path Destinations

Locorotondo: A Circular Beauty Locorotondo, located in the beautiful region of Puglia, Italy, is a captivating town known for its circular beauty. Nestled on a hilltop overlooking the picturesque Valle d'Itria, Locorotondo enchants visitors with its charming architecture, winding streets, and stunning panoramic views. The town's name, Locorotondo, translates to "round place," and it perfectly describes the unique layout and design of this enchanting destination. The historic center of Locorotondo is a labyrinth of narrow, whitewashed streets that form concentric circles, creating a circular pattern that is a feast for the eyes. As you stroll through Locorotondo's historic center, you'll be greeted by a succession of quaint alleys, adorned with flower-filled balconies, intricate wrought-iron balconies, and traditional stone buildings. The predominant color is dazzling white, which not only enhances the beauty of the town but also helps to keep it cool during the scorching summer months.

One of the most iconic features of Locorotondo is its unique roofscape. The roofs of the houses are characterized by "cummerse," traditional stone structures that form a sloping terrace and are often used for outdoor activities. From these rooftops, you can savor breathtaking vistas of the surrounding countryside, characterized by rolling hills, vineyards, and olive groves. Locorotondo is also renowned for its exceptional wine production. The town is located in the heart of the Valle d'Itria, a region celebrated for its high-quality wines, particularly the crisp white wines made from the Verdeca grape variety. Wine lovers can explore the local wineries, taste the delicious wines, and even participate in wine tours to learn about the winemaking process. Another highlight of Locorotondo is its rich cultural heritage. The town boasts several churches, such as the Chiesa Madre di San Giorgio and the Chiesa di San Rocco, displaying stunning baroque architecture and elaborate frescoes. Locorotondo is also known for its traditional festivals, including the vibrant "Locus Festival," which celebrates music and arts, attracting artists and performers from all over the world. Beyond the circular streets and cultural attractions, Locorotondo offers a serene and idyllic atmosphere that captures the essence of the Puglian way of life. The local cuisine is a gastronomic delight, with a focus on fresh, locally sourced ingredients. You can indulge in mouthwatering dishes like orecchiette pasta with tomato sauce, fava bean puree, and the famous Puglian burrata cheese. If you're seeking tranquility, Locorotondo serves as an excellent base for exploring the surrounding countryside. The nearby towns of Alberobello, famous for its trulli houses, and Martina Franca, with its elegant Baroque architecture, are just a short drive away. You can also venture further to discover the stunning Adriatic coastline, with its crystal-clear waters and charming seaside towns.

In conclusion, Locorotondo is a circular beauty in the heart of Puglia, Italy. Its circular streets, captivating architecture, panoramic views, and rich cultural heritage make it an irresistible destination for travelers. Whether you're seeking historical and architectural wonders, delightful cuisine, or a peaceful retreat surrounded by natural beauty, Locorotondo is sure to leave a lasting impression as you immerse yourself in its circular charm.

Cisternino: Charming Hilltop Town in puglia

Nestled in the picturesque region of Puglia in southern Italy, Cisternino stands as a charming hilltop town that captivates visitors with its enchanting beauty and rich history. With its whitewashed buildings, narrow winding streets, and panoramic views of the surrounding countryside, Cisternino offers a truly authentic and unforgettable Italian experience.One of the town's most striking features is its historic center, known as the "centro storico." Here, visitors can wander through narrow lanes adorned with vibrant flower pots and discover traditional stone houses, adorned with wrought-iron balconies and wooden shutters. The well-preserved architecture reflects Cisternino's past as a medieval town, transporting visitors back in time. One of the town's main attractions is the Piazza Vittorio Emanuele II, the central square that serves as the heart of Cisternino. This bustling square is a hub of activity, lined with cozy cafes, lively restaurants, and local shops. It's the perfect spot to relax, sip on a cup of espresso, and soak in the warm Mediterranean atmosphere while observing the friendly locals going about their daily routines.

Cisternino is also renowned for its unique trulli houses, traditional dry-stone dwellings with conical roofs. These iconic structures are scattered throughout the countryside surrounding the town, and many have been converted into charming accommodations for tourists seeking an authentic experience. Exploring the countryside and encountering these quaint trulli houses is a must-do when visiting Cisternino. Food lovers will find themselves in gastronomic heaven in Cisternino. The town is famous for its excellent cuisine, particularly its succulent grilled meats. The local butchers offer a unique experience, as visitors can choose their cuts of meat and have them cooked on-site. These "fornelli," or grills, are set up in the narrow streets, filling the air with tantalizing aromas. Pair your meal with a glass of local wine, and you'll have a true taste of Puglia.

For those seeking a bit of adventure, Cisternino is an excellent base for exploring the surrounding countryside. The rolling hills and olive groves provide the perfect setting for hiking or biking excursions. You can also take a leisurely drive through the countryside, passing by vineyards, ancient olive trees, and charming farms.

Cisternino's location in the heart of the Valle d'Itria makes it a convenient starting point for exploring other nearby towns. The enchanting Alberobello, famous for its UNESCO World Heritage-listed trulli village, is just a short drive away. The baroque beauty of Martina Franca and the whitewashed streets of Ostuni, known as the "White City," are also within easy reach. Whether you're drawn to its historical charm, delicious cuisine, or breathtaking scenery, Cisternino offers a truly enchanting experience in the heart of Puglia. Its blend of rich history, warm hospitality, and stunning landscapes make it a must-visit destination for travelers seeking an authentic taste of Italy's southern beauty.

Specchia: The Jewel of Salento

Specchia, often referred to as the "Jewel of Salento," is a captivating town located in the enchanting region of Puglia, Italy. Nestled amidst the rolling hills of the Salento Peninsula, this picturesque gem exudes an irresistible charm that captures the hearts of all who visit. With its rich history dating back to the Middle Ages, Specchia is a testament to the architectural and cultural heritage of the region. The town's historic center is a maze of narrow streets, alleys, and hidden corners, where time seems to stand still. As you wander through the cobblestone pathways, you'll encounter beautiful limestone buildings adorned with intricate carvings and wrought iron balconies, showcasing the skilled craftsmanship of the past.

The centerpiece of Specchia is undoubtedly its magnificent castle, known as Castello Risolo. This imposing fortress, perched atop a hill, offers panoramic views of the surrounding countryside. Built in the 14th century, it stands as a symbol of the town's medieval past and serves as a fascinating museum, housing artifacts and exhibits that depict the area's history. Another architectural masterpiece in Specchia is the Mother Church of Santa Eufemia. This stunning example of Baroque architecture boasts an ornate facade adorned with statues and intricate details. Step inside to discover a breathtaking interior, with its elegant frescoes, stucco decorations, and a beautiful marble altar. The church is a testament to the region's artistic heritage and provides a serene setting for reflection and contemplation. Beyond its architectural wonders, Specchia is also known for its vibrant cultural scene and warm hospitality. The town comes alive during the summer months with festivals, concerts, and cultural events that celebrate the traditions and customs of the Salento region. These festivities provide an opportunity to immerse yourself in the local culture, indulge in traditional cuisine, and witness colorful performances of traditional music and dance.

For nature enthusiasts, Specchia is an ideal base for exploring the pristine beaches and idyllic landscapes of Salento. Just a short drive away, you'll find the crystal-clear waters and sandy shores of the Ionian and Adriatic coasts. Whether you prefer lounging on sun-kissed beaches or embarking on scenic hikes along coastal trails, Specchia offers a gateway to some of Italy's most breathtaking natural beauty.

In addition to its natural and cultural wonders, Specchia boasts a gastronomic scene that tantalizes the taste buds. Indulge in the region's famous culinary delights, such as fresh seafood, locally produced olive oil, and delicious pasticciotti pastries. The town's restaurants and trattorias serve up authentic Puglian dishes that showcase the simplicity and flavors of the local ingredients.

As the sun sets over the rolling hills of Specchia, casting a golden glow upon its ancient walls, you'll understand why this town is considered a true treasure of Salento. Its timeless beauty, rich history, and warm hospitality make it a destination that leaves a lasting impression on every visitor. Whether you're seeking history, culture, nature, or simply a place to unwind and savor the finer things in life, Specchia beckons you to discover its undeniable charm and experience the essence of Puglia

Vieste: Stunning Coastal Town

Vieste, a stunning coastal town located in the Puglia region of Italy, is a true gem that captivates visitors with its natural beauty, rich history, and vibrant atmosphere. Situated on the easternmost point of the Gargano Peninsula, Vieste boasts breathtaking views of the Adriatic Sea, picturesque beaches, and a charming old town that exudes Mediterranean charm. One of the highlights of Vieste is its coastline, characterized by dramatic cliffs, hidden coves, and crystal-clear turquoise waters. The town is surrounded by a series of enchanting beaches, such as Pizzomunno Beach, known for its impressive limestone monolith that stands tall on the shore. Visitors can bask in the sun, take refreshing dips in the sea, or indulge in various water activities like snorkeling, kayaking, and sailing. Exploring the historic center of Vieste is like stepping back in time. As you stroll through the maze-like alleys, you'll discover quaint shops selling local handicrafts, delicious gelato stands, and cozy cafés where you can savor an espresso while enjoying the lively ambiance. Don't miss the chance to visit the beautiful Cathedral of Vieste, a striking example of Apulian Romanesque architecture. For panoramic views of the town and its surroundings, a visit to the Pizzomunno viewpoint is a must. From this vantage point, you can admire the rugged cliffs, the azure sea stretching as far as the eye can see, and the fascinating sea stacks that dot the coastline.

Nature enthusiasts will find plenty to explore in the vicinity of Vieste. The nearby Foresta Umbra, a vast forested area within the Gargano National Park, offers a tranquil retreat for hiking and wildlife spotting. You can also embark on a boat tour to explore the magnificent sea caves that lie along the coast, such as the famous Grotta dei Due Occhi (Cave of the Two Eyes).Vieste is also renowned for its delectable cuisine, which showcases the flavors of the region. Fresh seafood, locally produced olive oil, and aromatic herbs are just a few of the ingredients that make up the delicious dishes you can savor in the town's numerous trattorias and restaurants. Be sure to try the famous orecchiette pasta, a Puglian specialty, and indulge in some creamy gelato for a sweet ending to your meal. Whether you're seeking a relaxing beach getaway, a cultural exploration, or an outdoor adventure, Vieste has something to offer everyone. Its unspoiled natural beauty, charming historic center, and warm hospitality make it an unforgettable destination on the stunning coast of Puglia.

Altamura: Land of Bread and Caves

Altamura, located in the region of Puglia, Italy, is a captivating town renowned for its rich history, traditional bread, and fascinating underground caves. With its unique blend of ancient heritage and culinary delights, Altamura offers visitors a truly immersive and memorable experience. One of the most notable features of Altamura is its association with bread-making. The town has a long-standing reputation for producing exceptional bread, known as "Pane di Altamu.The baking process has remained unchanged for centuries, emphasizing the town's dedication to preserving culinary traditions. Walking through the streets of Altamura, you'll encounter numerous bakeries filling the air with the enticing aroma of freshly baked bread, inviting you to savor this local delicacy.

In addition to its bread-making heritage, Altamura is renowned for its fascinating underground caves. These caves, known as "Gravine," are a natural wonder and hold significant historical and archaeological value. Formed by erosion over thousands of years, the Gravine offer a glimpse into the region's ancient past. The caves were inhabited by prehistoric communities and later served as shelters for Byzantine monks. Exploring the Gravine provides a unique opportunity to witness the intricate network of cave dwellings and marvel at the natural beauty of the rock formations. Altamura's historical center is a captivating maze of narrow streets and picturesque squares, inviting visitors to take a leisurely stroll and soak in the town's ambiance. The focal point of the historical center is the magnificent Altamura Cathedral, an architectural masterpiece constructed in the 13th century. The cathedral showcases a blend of Romanesque and Gothic styles and houses a stunning collection of religious artworks. Its grandeur and historical significance make it a must-visit attraction in Altamura. Beyond its architectural wonders, Altamura offers a vibrant cultural scene. The town hosts various festivals and events throughout the year, celebrating its heritage and traditions. One such event is the "Sagra del Pane di Altamura," a festival dedicated to the famous bread of Altamura. During this festival, locals and visitors come together to appreciate the art of bread-making, indulge in delicious food, and enjoy live music and entertainment. Furthermore, Altamura's strategic location makes it an ideal base for exploring the stunning region of Puglia. Just a short drive away, you'll discover the UNESCO World Heritage site of Matera, renowned for its ancient cave dwellings known as "Sassi." The nearby picturesque towns of Alberobello and Polignano a Mare are also easily accessible, offering charming streets, breathtaking coastal views, and delectable cuisine. Altamura, with its land of bread and caves, provides a captivating blend of history, gastronomy, and natural beauty. Whether you're a history enthusiast, a food lover, or an avid adventurer, Altamura offers a remarkable experience that will leave an indelible mark on your journey through Puglia

Giovinazzo: Picturesque Fishing Village

Giovinazzo, a charming fishing village nestled along the Adriatic coast in the region of Puglia, Italy, is a hidden gem that captivates visitors with its picturesque beauty and authentic Italian charm. With its narrow, winding streets, historic architecture, and vibrant seafaring culture, Giovinazzo offers a unique and memorable experience for those seeking a tranquil escape. One of the most striking features of Giovinazzo is its idyllic harbor, which serves as the heart of the village. The harbor is filled with colorful fishing boats gently bobbing on the crystal-clear waters, creating a postcard-perfect scene. Stroll along the waterfront promenade, breathe in the fresh sea air, and watch as the fishermen bring in their daily catch. The harbor is not just a place of work but also a gathering spot for locals and visitors alike, where they can enjoy a leisurely coffee or indulge in the delicious seafood delicacies the village is known for. As you wander through the labyrinthine streets of Giovinazzo, you'll encounter a mix of medieval and Renaissance architecture. The village's historic center is a maze of narrow alleys, adorned with whitewashed houses, ornate balconies, and colorful flowers spilling over terracotta pots. The ancient walls that once protected the village still stand, evoking a sense of history and creating a distinctive ambiance. Explore the Piazza Vittorio Emanuele II, the main square, where you can admire the majestic Church of Santa Maria Assunta, a beautiful example of Apulian Romanesque architecture. Giovinazzo offers a multitude of cultural and culinary delights. Visit the Museo Civico, a small museum housed in a former palace, to discover the village's rich heritage and artistic treasures. The museum showcases archaeological artifacts, historical documents, and artworks, providing insight into Giovinazzo's past. Afterward, treat your taste buds to the delectable flavors of the local cuisine. The village is renowned for its fresh seafood, and you can savor a variety of dishes, from succulent octopus and grilled fish to creamy pasta dishes featuring the region's famous orecchiette.

For nature lovers, Giovinazzo is surrounded by stunning landscapes waiting to be explored. Take a leisurely stroll along the rocky coastline, breathe in the salty breeze, and marvel at the dramatic cliffs and hidden coves. If you're feeling more adventurous, head to nearby Torre Quetta, a sandy beach known for its clear waters, perfect for swimming and sunbathing. The pristine natural beauty of the area offers a serene retreat from the bustling cities and allows you to connect with the tranquil rhythm of coastal life.

Giovinazzo, with its captivating blend of history, scenic beauty, and authentic atmosphere, is a true gem in the crown of Puglia. Whether you're seeking a romantic getaway, a cultural exploration, or simply a place to unwind and enjoy the Mediterranean lifestyle, this picturesque fishing village is sure to leave a lasting impression. Immerse yourself in its timeless charm, indulge in the local traditions, and create unforgettable memories in the enchanting village of Giovinazzo.

Puglia's Art, Crafts, and Shopping

Puglia's Artistic Heritage

Puglia, located in the southern part of Italy, is renowned for its rich artistic heritage that spans centuries. The region is home to a diverse range of art forms, including architecture, sculpture, painting, and craftsmanship. Puglia's artistic heritage reflects its historical and cultural influences, resulting in a unique blend of styles and traditions. One of the most notable aspects of Puglia's artistic heritage is its architecture. The region is characterized by stunning examples of Romanesque, Gothic, and Baroque architecture. The city of Lecce, often referred to as the "Florence of the South," is famous for its elaborate Baroque buildings, featuring intricate facades adorned with ornate sculptures and decorative details. The Basilica of Santa Croce and the Church of Sant'Irene are prime examples of Lecce's architectural splendor. Another architectural gem in Puglia is the town of Alberobello, renowned for its trulli houses. These unique limestone dwellings with conical roofs are a UNESCO World Heritage site and have become an iconic symbol of the region. The trulli's simple yet fascinating design reflects the ingenuity of the local craftsmen who built them centuries ago. Puglia also boasts a vibrant tradition of sculpture. The region is home to several impressive sculptures, both ancient and modern. The bronze statue of Emperor Frederick II, located in the town of Altamura, is a remarkable example of medieval sculpture. The statue captures the powerful presence of the emperor, showcasing the artistic skills of the sculptor.

In addition to architecture and sculpture, Puglia has a long-standing tradition of painting. The region's art history is intertwined with the influence of renowned artists such as Francesco Solimena and Paolo Finoglio. Puglia's churches and museums house numerous masterpieces, including religious frescoes and altarpieces, which showcase the region's rich artistic legacy. Craftsmanship is yet another integral part of Puglia's artistic heritage. Skilled artisans in the region produce exquisite ceramics, intricate lacework, and vibrant textiles. The town of Grottaglie is particularly famous for its ceramics, which are highly prized for their craftsmanship and unique designs. Puglia's craftsmanship reflects a deep connection to the region's cultural roots and traditions. Puglia's artistic heritage is not limited to specific locations but permeates the entire region, contributing to its overall cultural identity. From the coastal towns with their colorful fishing boats and vibrant street art to the inland villages with their traditional crafts and architectural wonders, Puglia's artistic legacy is ever-present and offers a captivating glimpse into its history and culture.

Whether exploring the ancient streets of Lecce, admiring the trulli houses of Alberobello, or witnessing the intricate craftsmanship of Puglia's artisans, visitors are sure to be captivated by the region's artistic heritage. Puglia's art not only serves as a testament to the creativity and skill of its past inhabitants but also inspires and enriches the lives of those who encounter it today

Traditional Crafts and Artisans

Puglia, a region in southern Italy, is renowned for its rich cultural heritage, and traditional crafts and artisans play a significant role in preserving this legacy. The region boasts a long history of craftsmanship, with artisans passing down their skills and techniques from one generation to the next. From ceramics to textiles, woodworking to stone carving, Puglia is home to a diverse range of traditional crafts that showcase the creativity and craftsmanship of its people. Ceramics hold a special place in Puglia's artistic tradition. The town of Grottaglie is particularly famous for its ceramics, which have been produced there for centuries. Skilled artisans meticulously shape and decorate clay into beautiful pottery pieces, such as plates, bowls, jugs, and tiles. The vibrant colors and intricate patterns often depict traditional motifs, reflecting the region's history and culture.

Another remarkable craft in Puglia is textile production, notably the art of weaving. Looms can be found in various towns across the region, where artisans skillfully create fabrics using traditional techniques. These textiles are used for clothing, home furnishings, and tapestries. Alberobello, a UNESCO World Heritage site, is known for its exquisite embroideries, which feature delicate stitching and elaborate designs. Woodworking is yet another significant craft in Puglia. The town of Martina Franca is celebrated for its intricate woodcarvings. Skilled artisans carve wood into exquisite sculptures, furniture, and decorative items. Olive wood, in particular, is highly valued for its beautiful grain patterns and durability. Many artisans also create traditional musical instruments, such as tambourines and mandolins, showcasing the region's musical heritage.

Puglia's abundant limestone and marble deposits have given rise to a thriving stone carving industry. In Lecce, skilled stonemasons shape and sculpt stone to create intricate architectural details, statues, and ornamental pieces. The distinctive Baroque architecture of Lecce is adorned with the intricate craftsmanship of these artisans, making it a unique destination for admirers of stone carving.

In recent years, there has been a renewed interest in traditional crafts and a growing appreciation for the work of Puglia's artisans. Local initiatives and organizations have been established to support and promote these artisans, providing them with opportunities to showcase their work and connect with a broader audience. Craft fairs, exhibitions, and workshops are organized to celebrate the region's cultural heritage and encourage the continuation of traditional crafts.

The traditional crafts and artisans of Puglia are not only a testament to the region's artistic prowess but also contribute to its economy and cultural identity. These artisans preserve ancient techniques, often using locally sourced materials, and infuse their work with a sense of tradition and authenticity. By supporting these artisans and appreciating their craftsmanship, we can help ensure that these traditional crafts continue to thrive and pass on their legacy to future generations

Shopping in Puglia's Markets and Boutiques:

Puglia, located in southern Italy, is not only known for its stunning landscapes, rich history, and delicious cuisine but also for its vibrant shopping scene. The region offers a delightful mix of markets and boutiques where you can find unique local products, traditional crafts, and stylish fashion items. Let's take a closer look at shopping in Puglia's markets and boutiques.

Markets in Puglia: Puglia's markets are a treasure trove for those seeking authentic local experiences and traditional products. Here are some notable markets you should explore:

a. Lecce Market: The market in Lecce, the "Florence of the South," is a bustling hub of activity. Here, you'll find a wide range of goods, including fresh fruits and vegetables, locally produced cheeses, cured meats, olive oil, and wines.

Don't forget to haggle for the best prices and soak up the vibrant atmosphere.

b. Ostuni Market: Located in the picturesque white city of Ostuni, this market offers a blend of food, clothing, and household items. It's an excellent place to sample regional delicacies, such as taralli (a type of cracker) and locally grown olives. The market is held every Saturday and attracts locals and tourists alike.

c. Polignano a Mare Market: This coastal town is famous for its stunning cliffside views and charming market. Here, you can browse through stalls selling fresh seafood, locally made ceramics, handcrafted jewelry, and fashionable clothing. It's a great spot to find unique souvenirs to take home.

Boutiques in Puglia:

Puglia's boutiques are ideal for fashion enthusiasts and those looking for high-quality local products. The region's traditional craftsmanship and attention to detail shine through in these boutique offerings. They include:

a. **Bari's Old Town**: Bari, the capital of Puglia, boasts a charming old town packed with boutique shops. Explore the narrow streets and discover clothing boutiques featuring stylish Italian designs, leather goods, and accessories. You'll also find local artisans selling handmade ceramics, textiles, and intricate lacework.

b. **Martina Franca:** This picturesque town is renowned for its elegant Baroque architecture and its upscale boutiques. Martina Franca is particularly known for its high-quality fashion and jewelry. Take a leisurely stroll along the main shopping streets to discover unique pieces crafted by local artisans and designers.

c. **Alberobello**: Famous for its UNESCO World Heritage site of trulli houses, Alberobello is also home to shops specializing in trulli-inspired souvenirs. These traditional cone-shaped dwellings have inspired local artisans to create miniature trulli crafts, ceramics, and other decorative items that make for distinctive keepsakes. Whether you're hunting for culinary delights, fashionable clothing, or traditional crafts, Puglia's markets and boutiques provide a delightful shopping experience. Remember to explore the local specialties and engage with the friendly shopkeepers, as they often have fascinating stories to share about their products and the region's cultural heritage

Souvenirs and Local Handicrafts

Puglia, located in the southern part of Italy, is a region known for its stunning landscapes, rich history, and vibrant culture. One aspect of Puglia that captivates visitors is its wide array of souvenirs and local handicrafts. From traditional ceramics to intricate lacework, Puglia offers a treasure trove of unique and authentic crafts that make for perfect mementos or gifts. Let's explore some of the popular souvenirs and local handicrafts you can find in Puglia.

Ceramics: Puglia is renowned for its beautiful ceramics, which reflect the region's artistic heritage. The town of Grottaglie is particularly famous for its pottery tradition. You can find intricately painted plates, bowls, vases, and tiles adorned with vibrant colors and traditional patterns. The craftsmanship and attention to detail make these ceramics highly sought after.

Taralli: Taralli are a type of crunchy snack that is emblematic of Puglia. These ring-shaped biscuits are made from simple ingredients like flour, olive oil, and white wine, and are often flavored with fennel seeds or black pepper. Taralli come in various sizes and flavors, and they are not only delicious but also make for a great edible souvenir to take back home.

Olive Wood Products: Puglia is famous for its olive groves, and artisans in the region skillfully craft olive wood into unique and functional items. From cutting boards and salad bowls to utensils and kitchenware, olive wood products are not only visually appealing but also durable and long-lasting. They provide a rustic touch to any home and serve as a reminder of Puglia's strong connection to olive cultivation.

Pizzo Lace: The town of Pizzo in Puglia is renowned for its delicate lacework, known as "Pizzo di Cantù." This intricate and meticulously crafted lace has a long history and is highly regarded for its beauty and quality. You can find Pizzo lace in various forms, including tablecloths, doilies, handkerchiefs, and even clothing. These exquisite lace products are cherished souvenirs that showcase the region's artisanal skills.

Olive Oil: Puglia is one of Italy's major producers of olive oil, and the region's olive oil is highly regarded for its superior quality. Considered the "liquid gold" of Puglia, a bottle of extra virgin olive oil from the region makes for an excellent souvenir. Look for bottles labeled "DOP" (Protected Designation of Origin) to ensure authenticity and the highest standards.

Hand-Painted Fans: Puglia's hot summers have given rise to the tradition of hand-painted fans. These beautifully decorated fans are not only practical for keeping cool but also serve as decorative pieces. You can find fans adorned with vibrant floral patterns, traditional motifs, or even scenes depicting Puglia's landscapes and landmarks.

When visiting Puglia, exploring the local markets, boutiques, and artisan workshops is the best way to discover these authentic souvenirs and local handicrafts. Not only do these items make for memorable keepsakes, but they also support local artisans and preserve the region's cultural heritage

Puglia's Street Markets and Flea Markets

Puglia, located in the southern part of Italy, is not only known for its stunning beaches and rich cultural heritage but also for its vibrant street markets and flea markets. These markets offer a unique shopping experience where locals and visitors can immerse themselves in the region's traditional crafts, delicious food, and lively atmosphere. Let's explore some of the popular street markets and flea markets in Puglia.

Lecce Market: Lecce, known as the "Florence of the South," hosts a bustling street market every Sunday. This market is a treasure trove of local products, from fresh fruits and vegetables to cheese, olive oil, and local wines. As you stroll through the market, the aroma of freshly brewed coffee and street food will tempt your taste buds.

Taranto Fish Market: Taranto, a coastal city, boasts a vibrant fish market that is a must-visit for seafood lovers. Located near the waterfront, this market is known for its wide variety of freshly caught fish and shellfish. The colorful display of seafood, the shouts of fishermen, and the lively atmosphere create an authentic experience. You can purchase the catch of the day and even have it cooked at nearby restaurants.

Martina Franca Flea Market: Martina Franca, a picturesque town in the Itria Valley, hosts a popular flea market on the third Sunday of every month. This market is a treasure trove for antique enthusiasts and collectors. You can find a wide range of items, including vintage furniture, ceramics, paintings, books, and unique handicrafts. Exploring the market is like stepping back in time and uncovering hidden gems.

Bari Mercato Coperto: Bari, the capital of Puglia, is home to the Mercato Coperto, a covered market that offers an authentic culinary experience. Here, you can find an array of fresh produce, including fruits, vegetables, meats, cheeses, and seafood. Don't miss the chance to sample local delicacies like orecchiette pasta, burrata cheese, and taralli (savory biscuits). The market is a bustling hub of activity, with vendors showcasing their goods and locals haggling for the best prices.

Ostuni Market: Ostuni, often called the "White City" due to its whitewashed buildings, hosts a vibrant weekly market on Saturdays. This market offers a wide variety of goods, ranging from clothing and accessories to local food products. It's a great place to buy souvenirs, handmade crafts, and traditional Puglian ceramics. As you browse through the stalls, you can savor the aroma of freshly baked bread and taste local specialties.

These are just a few examples of the many street markets and flea markets you can find in Puglia. Each market has its own charm and reflects the unique character of the region. Whether you're looking for fresh ingredients, unique crafts, or a taste of local culture, Puglia's street markets and flea markets are sure to delight your senses and provide an unforgettable experience

Antique Hunting and Vintage Shopping

Antique hunting and vintage shopping in Puglia, Italy, offer a delightful experience for those seeking unique treasures and a glimpse into the region's rich history. Puglia, located in the southern part of Italy, is renowned for its beautiful landscapes, charming towns, and a cultural heritage that spans centuries. Exploring its antique markets, vintage shops, and hidden gems can be a fascinating journey back in time. One of the most prominent antique markets in Puglia is the Mercatino dell'Antiquariato di Lecce. Held in the picturesque city of Lecce, this market takes place on the last Sunday of every month and attracts antique enthusiasts from far and wide. Strolling through the market, visitors can find a diverse range of items, including furniture, artwork, ceramics, jewelry, and vintage clothing. It's an ideal place to discover unique pieces that reflect the artistic and cultural heritage of the region.

Another noteworthy destination for antique hunting in Puglia is the city of Ostuni. This charming town boasts a rich history and is home to several antique shops that cater to collectors and vintage lovers. Exploring the narrow alleys and cobblestone streets, visitors can stumble upon hidden boutiques and galleries that showcase an array of antique furniture, lighting fixtures, and decorative items. The timeless beauty of Ostuni serves as a perfect backdrop for finding one-of-a-kind pieces to adorn your home or add to your collection.

In addition to these established markets and shops, Puglia also offers a unique experience in the form of "mammoth markets." These are large-scale, open-air markets that combine elements of flea markets, antique fairs, and general shopping. These mammoth markets often take place in different towns across Puglia on specific dates throughout the year. They offer a treasure trove of antiques, vintage items, and curiosities, ranging from furniture and textiles to vintage toys and kitchenware. Exploring these markets can be an exciting adventure, as you never know what hidden gems you might come across. Beyond the organized markets and shops, Puglia is a region that rewards the curious explorer. Many small towns and villages have local artisans and craftsmen who specialize in restoring and selling antiques. These artisans often have their workshops tucked away in historic buildings, and visiting them can be an opportunity to witness traditional techniques and learn about the history of the pieces they work on. Engaging with these artisans not only allows you to find unique pieces but also creates a connection to the local culture and craftsmanship of Puglia. When embarking on an antique hunting or vintage shopping adventure in Puglia, it's essential to keep an open mind and be prepared to explore off-the-beaten-path locations. From small family-run shops to bustling markets and encounters with local artisans, the region offers a rich tapestry of opportunities for collectors, enthusiasts, and anyone seeking a unique piece of history. As with any antique shopping experience, it's important to exercise caution and ensure the authenticity and quality of the items you're interested in. Familiarize yourself with the history and characteristics of the objects you're seeking, and if needed, consult with local experts or appraisers to make informed decisions.

In conclusion, antique hunting and vintage shopping in Puglia provide a delightful blend of history, culture, and unique finds. Whether you're a passionate collector or simply love discovering timeless treasures, Puglia's markets, shops, and hidden gems offer a rewarding experience that connects you with the region's rich past and vibrant present.

Practical Information for Travelers

Accommodation Options in Puglia: Puglia, located in the southern region of Italy, is a stunning destination known for its picturesque coastline, charming towns, and rich cultural heritage. When it comes to accommodation options, Puglia offers a wide range of choices to suit every traveler's preferences and budget. Whether you're looking for luxury resorts, boutique hotels, cozy bed and breakfasts, or self-catering villas, Puglia has something to offer for everyone. Here are some popular accommodation options in Puglia:

Masserie: Puglia is famous for its masserie, traditional fortified farmhouses that have been converted into luxury accommodations. These properties typically feature beautiful gardens, swimming pools, and elegant rooms. Staying in a masseria allows you to experience the region's rustic charm while enjoying modern amenities and impeccable service.

Trulli: Another unique accommodation option in Puglia is the trullo. Trulli are traditional dry stone huts with conical roofs, characteristic of the Itria Valley. Many trulli have been renovated and transformed into comfortable holiday homes, offering a cozy and authentic experience. Alberobello is the most famous town for trulli accommodation, but you can find them in other areas of Puglia as well.

Luxury Resorts: Puglia boasts several luxury resorts along its beautiful coastline. These resorts offer high-end amenities such as private beaches, spa facilities, golf courses, and fine dining options. Many of them also provide organized activities and excursions, ensuring a memorable and indulgent stay.

Boutique Hotels: Puglia is home to numerous boutique hotels, often located in historic buildings or charming seaside towns. These hotels provide a personalized and intimate atmosphere, with stylishly designed rooms and attentive service. They are perfect for travelers seeking a unique and authentic experience.

Bed and Breakfasts: Puglia has an abundance of bed and breakfast accommodations, particularly in its historic towns. These establishments offer comfortable rooms with breakfast included, and they often have a warm and welcoming ambiance. Staying in a bed and breakfast allows you to immerse yourself in the local culture and receive personalized recommendations from the hosts.

Self-Catering Villas: If you prefer more independence and privacy, renting a self-catering villa in Puglia might be the ideal option for you. Puglia has an array of villas available for short-term rentals, ranging from small countryside retreats to lavish seaside estates. These villas usually come with fully equipped kitchens, private pools, and outdoor spaces, giving you the freedom to relax and enjoy your vacation at your own pace.

Whether you choose to stay in a luxury resort, a traditional trullo, or a charming bed and breakfast, Puglia offers a wealth of accommodation options that cater to different preferences. With its natural beauty, historical sites, and delectable cuisine, Puglia provides an unforgettable Italian experience for visitors from around the world

Transportation and Getting Around Puglia :

Puglia, located in southern Italy, is a beautiful and vibrant region known for its stunning coastline, picturesque towns, and rich cultural heritage. When it comes to getting around and exploring this enchanting destination, Puglia offers various transportation options to suit different preferences and needs. Whether you're planning to visit the historical sites in Bari, relax on the beaches of Salento, or delve into the charming towns of Alberobello and Ostuni, here is a guide to transportation in Puglia.

Air Travel: Puglia has three major airports: Bari Karol Wojtyła Airport, Brindisi Airport, and Foggia "Gino Lisa" Airport. These airports are well-connected to major Italian and European cities, making air travel a convenient option for reaching Puglia. Upon arrival, you can rent a car or take advantage of other transportation modes available to explore the region.

Train: The train network in Puglia is efficient and connects various towns and cities within the region. The main railway line, known as the Adriatic Railway Line, runs along the eastern coast of Puglia, connecting cities such as Bari, Brindisi, and Lecce. The Ferrovie del Sud Est (FSE) railway also operates in the region, providing connections to smaller towns and villages. Trains are a convenient and comfortable way to travel between destinations in Puglia, offering scenic views of the countryside along the way.

Bus: Buses are a popular mode of transportation for both short and long distances in Puglia. The regional bus company, Ferrovie del Sud Est (FSE), operates an extensive network of buses that connect various towns and villages throughout the region. Additionally, private bus companies provide intercity and regional bus services, offering convenient connections between major cities and tourist destinations in Puglia.

Car Rental: Renting a car is a popular choice for exploring Puglia independently. All major cities and airports in the region have car rental services available. Having a car gives you the freedom to explore at your own pace, visit off-the-beaten-path destinations, and access remote areas that might be harder to reach by public transportation. However, it's important to note that some towns, especially historic centers, have limited or restricted car access due to narrow streets and pedestrian zones. Parking may also be a challenge in popular tourist areas, so it's advisable to plan accordingly.

Cycling: Puglia offers a delightful cycling experience, with its flat terrain and scenic landscapes. Several companies and local organizations provide bicycle rentals and organized cycling tours, allowing you to explore the region at a leisurely pace. Cycling is an excellent way to immerse yourself in the beauty of Puglia's countryside, discover hidden gems, and experience the authentic charm of the region.

Ferry hubs: Puglia's coastal location offers opportunities for ferry travel, particularly to and from neighboring regions and countries. The ports of Bari and Brindisi are major ferry hubs, providing connections to destinations such as Greece, Croatia, and Albania. Ferry services offer a unique and scenic way to travel, especially for those interested in island hopping or combining their Puglia visit with other Mediterranean destinations.

In conclusion, Puglia provides various transportation options to suit different preferences and needs. Whether you prefer the convenience of air travel, the flexibility of a rental car, or the charm of exploring by train, bus, or bicycle, you can easily navigate the region and discover its many treasures. Choose the mode of transportation that best suits your itinerary and embark on a memorable journey through the enchanting region of Puglia

Health and Safety Tips

Health and safety should always be a top priority when traveling, and Puglia, a beautiful region in southern Italy, is no exception. Here are some essential health and safety tips to keep in mind during your visit to Puglia:

Stay Hydrated: Puglia experiences hot and sunny summers, so it's crucial to stay hydrated. Carry a water bottle with you at all times and drink plenty of fluids, especially during peak daytime hours. Dehydration can lead to fatigue and other health issues, so ensure you have access to clean drinking water.

Protect Yourself from the Sun: When exploring Puglia's stunning beaches, charming towns, and scenic countryside, protect your skin from the sun's harmful rays. Apply sunscreen with a high SPF, wear a hat, sunglasses, and lightweight, loose-fitting clothing that covers your skin. Seek shade during the hottest part of the day to avoid sunburn and heatstroke.

Practice Food and Water Safety: Puglia is renowned for its delicious cuisine, but it's essential to prioritize food and water safety. Opt for bottled or purified water and avoid consuming tap water unless it has been properly treated. When dining out, choose reputable restaurants with good hygiene practices, and ensure your food is cooked thoroughly, particularly meat and seafood.

Mosquito Protection: Like many warm regions, Puglia is home to mosquitoes, especially during the summer months. Protect yourself from mosquito bites by using insect repellent containing DEET, wearing long sleeves and pants during the evenings, and using mosquito nets or screens when necessary, especially in accommodations without air conditioning.

Road Safety: If you plan on renting a car or using local transportation, be mindful of road safety. Familiarize yourself with local traffic rules, follow speed limits, and drive defensively. Be cautious when crossing the road, and always use designated pedestrian crossings where available. It's also a good idea to have travel insurance that covers medical emergencies and accidents.

Stay Vigilant against Petty Theft: Puglia, like many tourist destinations, may have incidents of petty theft. Protect your belongings by being mindful of your surroundings and avoiding crowded areas where pickpockets might operate. Use a money belt or a secure bag to keep your valuables close to you, and never leave your belongings unattended, particularly in busy tourist spots.

Stay Informed about COVID-19: Stay up to date with the latest travel advisories and guidelines regarding COVID-19. Follow any local regulations, wear face masks in crowded areas or when required, practice good hand hygiene, and maintain social distancing where necessary. It's also advisable to carry hand sanitizer with you for occasions when soap and water are not readily available. Remember, these tips are general guidelines, and it's always a good idea to consult official travel resources, such as government websites or local tourism authorities, for the most accurate and up-to-date information on health and safety precautions in Puglia. Enjoy your trip while prioritizing your well-being

Language and Communication

Puglia, located in southern Italy, is a region rich in history, culture, and natural beauty. As with any region, language and communication play an important role in shaping the identity and character of the area. In Puglia, a distinct dialect and unique linguistic heritage have developed over centuries, contributing to the region's vibrant linguistic landscape. The primary language spoken in Puglia is Italian, the official language of Italy. Italian serves as the standard form of communication in government, education, and formal settings. However, like many regions in Italy, Puglia has its own distinct dialect known as "Pugliese" or "Puglian dialect." The Pugliese dialect is a variant of the broader Southern Italian dialects, influenced by the region's historical and cultural interactions. It carries traces of the ancient Greek language spoken by the Greek colonists who settled in Puglia during ancient times. Additionally, due to Puglia's strategic location as a crossroads between the Mediterranean and other regions of Italy, the dialect incorporates elements from other languages, such as Arabic, French, and Spanish.

The Pugliese dialect reflects the region's unique character and is an essential part of the local culture. It is often heard in informal conversations, gatherings, and in more rural areas. Locals use the dialect to express their identity, connect with their heritage, and establish a sense of belonging within the community. The Pugliese dialect serves as a linguistic bridge between generations, preserving traditions, folklore, and local expressions that might otherwise be lost. Furthermore, Puglia's rich history and diverse cultural influences have shaped its linguistic landscape. The region's coastal areas have been home to Greek-speaking populations for centuries, leading to the preservation of Greek dialects in some villages, especially in Salento. The presence of Greek, Albanian, and other minority languages highlights the linguistic diversity within Puglia.

In recent years, the role of English as an international language has also become more prominent in Puglia, driven by the growth of tourism and international business. English is commonly spoken in tourist areas, hotels, and restaurants to accommodate visitors from around the world. Many locals, especially younger generations, have embraced English as a means to engage with a global audience and enhance their professional opportunities. In terms of written communication, Italian is the standard language used in official documents, education, and media. However, Puglia also boasts a rich literary tradition, with authors and poets who have contributed to the region's cultural heritage. Some have chosen to write in the Pugliese dialect, showcasing the expressive potential and beauty of the local language.

In conclusion, language and communication in Puglia are diverse and dynamic, reflecting the region's historical, cultural, and linguistic influences. Italian serves as the official language, while the Pugliese dialect and its variants play a significant role in local identity and cultural expression. The region's linguistic landscape is further enriched by the presence of minority languages and the growing importance of English as an international means of communication. Language in Puglia is not only a tool for everyday interactions but also a key element in preserving traditions, connecting with the past, and forging a sense of community

Currency and Banking

Puglia, a beautiful region located in southern Italy, has a well-established currency and banking system. As part of Italy, Puglia uses the Euro (€) as its official currency, just like the rest of the country and most other nations within the Eurozone. The Euro is a widely accepted and stable currency, facilitating economic transactions within Puglia and throughout the European Union. In Puglia, as in other regions of Italy, banking services are readily available and cater to the financial needs of residents, businesses, and tourists. Both national and international banks have a presence in Puglia, offering a range of services such as personal and business accounts, loans, mortgages, and investment opportunities.

Major Italian banks, such as UniCredit, Intesa Sanpaolo, and Banco BPM, have branches in various cities and towns across Puglia. Additionally, there are smaller local banks and cooperative banks that serve the needs of specific communities within the region.

ATMs (Automated Teller Machines) are widespread in Puglia, allowing residents and visitors to withdraw cash and conduct basic banking transactions. These ATMs usually support multiple languages, including English, making it convenient for tourists to access their accounts.

When it comes to online banking, Puglia's banks provide secure and user-friendly internet banking platforms. Customers can access their accounts, transfer funds, pay bills, and perform other transactions conveniently from their computers or mobile devices. In recent years, digital payment options, such as mobile payment apps and contactless payments, have gained popularity in Italy, including Puglia. Major credit cards like Visa and Mastercard are widely accepted in most establishments, including hotels, restaurants, and retail stores. Puglia, being a popular tourist destination, also has currency exchange services available at airports, major cities, and tourist areas.

Travelers can exchange their foreign currency for Euros to meet their financial needs during their visit. Overall, Puglia benefits from a robust banking system and a widely accepted currency, the Euro. Whether you are a resident, a business owner, or a visitor to Puglia, you will find a range of banking services and convenient payment options to meet your financial requirements in the region

Local Etiquette and Customs

Puglia, located in southern Italy, is known for its rich history, stunning landscapes, and vibrant culture. When visiting Puglia, it is important to familiarize yourself with the local etiquette and customs to ensure a respectful and enjoyable experience. Some key aspect includes:

Greetings and Personal Space: Italians are generally warm and friendly, so don't be surprised if people greet you with a kiss on both cheeks, even if they are meeting you for the first time. Handshakes are also common. Italians appreciate personal space, so maintain a comfortable distance during conversations.

Dress Code: Puglia has a relaxed atmosphere, but it is advisable to dress modestly and respectfully, especially when visiting churches or religious sites. Avoid wearing beachwear or revealing clothing in such places. Dressing elegantly, especially during evening outings, is appreciated.

Punctuality: Italians have a more relaxed approach to time, so being fashionably late for social gatherings is generally acceptable. However, it is still advisable to be punctual for business appointments or formal events.

Dining Etiquette: When dining in Puglia, expect meals to be a leisurely affair. Italians take their food seriously and appreciate good company and conversation during meals. Keep in mind that many Italians are passionate about their local cuisine, so be open to trying traditional Puglian dishes and savoring each course.

Respect for Cultural Sites: Puglia is home to numerous historical and religious sites, such as cathedrals, castles, and archaeological sites. When visiting these places, show respect by observing any rules or dress codes in place. Avoid touching or damaging any artifacts or structures, and keep noise levels to a minimum.

Tipping: Tipping in Puglia follows the general practice in Italy. A service charge is often included in the bill, but leaving a small tip for exceptional service is appreciated. It is customary to round up the bill or leave a few euros on the table.

Language: While many Italians in Puglia speak English, it is always appreciated when visitors make an effort to speak a few basic Italian phrases. Simple greetings and expressions of gratitude can go a long way in fostering positive interactions.

Festivals and Events: Puglia is renowned for its vibrant festivals and events throughout the year. If you happen to attend one, respect the local traditions and customs associated with the celebration. Be mindful of any religious or cultural significance and participate with enthusiasm and respect. By embracing the local etiquette and customs in Puglia, you will not only have a more enriching experience but also show respect for the local culture and traditions. Enjoy your time exploring the beautiful region of Puglia

Puglia's Day Trips and Nearby Excursions

Matera and the Sassi Cave Dwellings

Matera and the Sassi Cave Dwellings are captivating historical and cultural sites located in the region of Basilicata, Italy. While Matera itself is not in Puglia, it is situated close to the border of Puglia and is often included in travel itineraries for visitors exploring the region. Let's delve into the fascinating history and significance of Matera and the Sassi Cave Dwellings. Matera, often referred to as "la Città Sotterranea" (the Underground City), is one of the oldest continuously inhabited settlements in the world. Its history can be traced back to the Paleolithic era, making it over 9,000 years old. The city's unique charm lies in its ancient cave dwellings, known as the Sassi, which are carved into the rock formations of the Murgia plateau. The Sassi Cave Dwellings are a remarkable example of human adaptation to a challenging environment.

The caves were originally natural formations, but over time, the inhabitants excavated and transformed them into homes, churches, and other structures. These cave dwellings allowed the local communities to survive and thrive in this rugged terrain. The Sassi are divided into two distinct areas: Sasso Caveoso and Sasso Barisano. Sasso Caveoso, the oldest part, features a labyrinthine network of cave dwellings, narrow streets, and staircases. Sasso Barisano, on the other hand, showcases a more urbanized area with multi-story cave dwellings and stunning views over the city. For centuries, Matera and its Sassi were impoverished and neglected, suffering from unsanitary conditions and poverty. However, in the mid-20th century, the Italian government took notice of the dire situation and initiated a restoration project. The people who were living in the Sassi were relocated, and the area underwent extensive renovation, transforming it into the UNESCO World Heritage site that it is today. The restoration of Matera and the Sassi Cave Dwellings has not only preserved an extraordinary historical site but also rejuvenated the city. Today, visitors can explore the ancient cave houses, visit museums that depict the life of the past, and even stay in converted cave hotels, offering a unique and immersive experience.

The haunting beauty of Matera and its Sassi has also captured the attention of filmmakers. The city has served as a backdrop for numerous movies, including Mel Gibson's "The Passion of the Christ" and more recently, the James Bond film "No Time to Die." The enchanting ambiance and timeless quality of Matera's streets and caves make it a captivating setting for cinematic storytelling.

Matera and the Sassi Cave Dwellings are not only an archaeological treasure but also a symbol of human resilience and ingenuity. The site stands as a testament to the ability of communities to adapt and flourish even in the most challenging circumstances. It is a place where ancient history merges with contemporary life, inviting visitors to step back in time and appreciate the remarkable cultural heritage of this unique region.

Castellana Grotte: Underground Wonders in puglia

Introduction:

Nestled in the picturesque region of Puglia, Italy, lies a hidden gem that takes visitors on a remarkable journey beneath the earth's surface. Castellana Grotte, a small town in the province of Bari, is renowned for its awe-inspiring underground caves. This subterranean wonderland offers a captivating blend of natural beauty, geological formations, and rich history, making it a must-visit destination for adventure seekers and nature enthusiasts alike.

Unveiling the Spectacular Caves: The star attraction of Castellana Grotte is undoubtedly the Grotte di Castellana, a complex of underground caves that stretches for over three kilometers. These magnificent caves were formed over millions of years through a slow but steady process of water erosion. Visitors can embark on guided tours that lead them through a series of stunning chambers, each with its own unique charm. As visitors venture deeper into the Grotte di Castellana, they are greeted by a mesmerizing display of stalactites, stalagmites, and intricate rock formations. These natural works of art, formed drop by drop over centuries, create a surreal and otherworldly atmosphere. The caves' vastness and the ethereal play of light and shadows add to the sense of enchantment, leaving visitors in awe of nature's grandeur.

The Grave of the White Cave Bear:

One of the most intriguing features of the Grotte di Castellana is the discovery of the remains of Ursus spelaeus, or the White Cave Bear, an extinct species that lived during the Ice Age. The presence of these fossils adds a touch of mystery to the caves, connecting visitors to an ancient era long gone. It serves as a reminder of the immense geological and historical significance of this underground wonderland.

Historical Significance: Beyond their natural beauty, the caves of Castellana also hold historical importance. In World War II, they served as a refuge for locals during bombings, with their extensive underground network providing shelter and safety. Exploring these caves not only unveils their geological secrets but also offers a glimpse into the resilience and ingenuity of the people who sought solace within their depths.

Exploring Above Ground: While the underground caves steal the spotlight, Castellana Grotte also offers above-ground attractions. The town itself boasts a charming atmosphere, with traditional stone houses, winding streets, and welcoming locals. Visitors can take leisurely strolls through the town, indulge in authentic Italian cuisine, and immerse themselves in the warmth of the local culture.

Preservation and Sustainability: Preservation and sustainability are paramount when it comes to protecting the fragile underground ecosystem of Castellana Grotte. Efforts are made to maintain the caves in their natural state, ensuring that future generations can continue to appreciate their beauty. Responsible tourism practices, such as guided tours and educational initiatives, promote an understanding of the delicate balance between human interaction and environmental conservation.

Conclusion: castellana Grotte's underground wonders in Puglia are a testament to the extraordinary beauty that lies beneath the Earth's surface. The Grotte di Castellana offer a surreal experience, where visitors can marvel at nature's artistry and uncover ancient secrets. This subterranean wonderland, combined with the charm of the surrounding town, creates an unforgettable journey for those who venture into the depths of Castellana Grotte.

Taranto and the Archaeological Sites

Taranto is a captivating city located in the region of Puglia, in southern Italy. Renowned for its rich history and remarkable archaeological sites, Taranto offers visitors a unique glimpse into the ancient civilizations that once thrived in the area.

One of the most prominent archaeological sites in Taranto is the Taranto National Archaeological Museum. Housed in a former convent, the museum showcases a vast collection of artifacts from different historical periods, including the impressive treasures of ancient Greek colonies that once existed in Taranto. Visitors can admire exquisite gold jewelry, intricately decorated pottery, and sculptures that offer insights into the lives of the ancient inhabitants. Another fascinating site in Taranto is the Old Town, also known as the "Città Vecchia." This area encompasses a maze of narrow streets and alleys, dotted with historical buildings, churches, and quaint piazzas. Walking through the Old Town feels like stepping back in time, with its charming atmosphere and well-preserved architecture.

Heading outside of Taranto, Puglia offers several other remarkable archaeological sites. One of the most remarkable is the UNESCO World Heritage Site of Alberobello, famous for its unique trulli houses. These traditional cone-shaped buildings with whitewashed walls and stone roofs create a surreal landscape, evoking a sense of magic and wonder. Exploring the narrow streets of Alberobello is like venturing into a fairytale village frozen in time. In the town of Ostuni, known as the "White City," visitors can discover a blend of history and breathtaking views. Perched on a hilltop, the old town of Ostuni is characterized by its whitewashed buildings, narrow staircases, and charming squares. The Cathedral of Ostuni, an impressive example of Gothic-Romanesque architecture, stands as a prominent landmark and offers a glimpse into the town's historical and cultural significance.

Further south, the archaeological park of Egnazia near Fasano showcases the ruins of an ancient

Messapian and Roman city. Visitors can explore the remains of streets, houses, temples, and even a Roman amphitheater. The site provides a fascinating insight into the civilizations that once occupied this area and their architectural achievements. Puglia, with its abundance of archaeological sites and historical treasures, offers a captivating journey through time. From the ancient Greek colonies in Taranto to the fairytale-like trulli houses of Alberobello and the historical charm of Ostuni, this region provides a unique opportunity to immerse oneself in the rich history and cultural heritage of southern Italy

Foggia and the Gargano National Park

Foggia and the Gargano National Park are two prominent destinations located in the beautiful region of Puglia, Italy. Let's delve into each of these places and discover what makes them special. Foggia is a historic city situated in the northern part of Puglia. It is known for its rich agricultural landscape, vibrant culture, and fascinating history. Foggia has a strategic location on the Tavoliere, a vast plain that is considered the "granary of Italy" due to its fertile soil. The city has a long history that dates back to ancient times, and it has been influenced by various civilizations throughout the centuries, including the Greeks, Romans, and Normans. One of the most iconic landmarks in Foggia is the Cathedral of Foggia, also known as the Cattedrale di Santa Maria Icona Vetere. This magnificent cathedral showcases a blend of architectural styles, with elements from the Romanesque, Gothic, and Baroque periods. Inside, visitors can admire beautiful frescoes and intricate artwork. Foggia is also famous for its culinary delights. The region is renowned for its excellent olive oil, which is produced from the abundant olive groves surrounding the city. Additionally, Foggia is known for its traditional dishes, such as orecchiette pasta with broccoli rabe, lamb dishes, and various types of cheese. Exploring the local markets and restaurants is a must for food enthusiasts visiting Foggia. Now let's turn our attention to the Gargano National Park, a stunning natural reserve located in the province of Foggia. The park covers a vast area encompassing the Gargano Peninsula, the spur of Italy's boot-shaped land. It is a place of exceptional beauty, characterized by diverse landscapes ranging from rugged cliffs and picturesque beaches to lush forests and enchanting lakes. The Gargano National Park is a paradise for outdoor enthusiasts and nature lovers. It offers a wide range of activities, including hiking, mountain biking, birdwatching, and boating. The park is home to several trails that wind through its breathtaking scenery, leading visitors to discover hidden grottoes, ancient forests, and panoramic viewpoints. One of the park's most iconic attractions is the Foresta Umbra, a dense forest covering an area of approximately 11,000 hectares. This ancient woodland is home to a remarkable variety of flora and fauna, including centuries-old beech trees, wild orchids, and rare bird species. Exploring the Foresta Umbra is like stepping into a fairytale forest, with its tranquil atmosphere and natural wonders. Along the coast of the Gargano Peninsula, visitors can find stunning beaches and crystal-clear waters. The coastline is dotted with charming seaside towns, such as Vieste and Peschici, offering picturesque landscapes, vibrant local culture, and delicious seafood.

In addition to its natural beauty, the Gargano National Park is also home to several cultural and historical sites. The Sanctuary of Monte Sant'Angelo, a UNESCO World Heritage site, is a significant pilgrimage destination due to its association with the archangel Michael. The sanctuary is perched on a rocky hilltop and offers panoramic views of the surrounding landscape.

In conclusion, Foggia and the Gargano National Park in Puglia, Italy, offer a captivating blend of history, natural beauty, and culinary delights. Whether you're exploring the ancient streets of Foggia or immersing yourself in the stunning landscapes of the Gargano National Park, these destinations are sure to leave a lasting impression on any traveler seeking an authentic Italian experience.

Trulli of Alberobello and Locorotondo

The Trulli of Alberobello and the town of Locorotondo are two captivating destinations in the region of Puglia, Italy, known for their unique architectural beauty and rich cultural heritage. Let's delve into the enchanting world of these two remarkable places.

The Trulli of Alberobello: Alberobello, a small town located in the Itria Valley of Puglia, is renowned for its extraordinary collection of trulli. Trulli are traditional Apulian houses made of limestone and characterized by their conical roofs. The trulli of Alberobello have become an iconic symbol of the region, attracting visitors from all over the world. These distinctive dwellings were built without the use of mortar, with each trullo consisting of a circular base and a conical roof made of stacked stone slabs. The trulli were originally constructed in the 14th century and have since been recognized as a UNESCO World Heritage site due to their exceptional architectural value. Walking through the streets of Alberobello, visitors will find themselves immersed in a fairy-tale-like atmosphere. The town is divided into two main areas: Rione Monti and Aia Piccola. Rione Monti is the larger district, home to the majority of trulli. It boasts narrow cobblestone streets lined with whitewashed trulli, adorned with distinctive symbols and mystical religious markings. The Aia Piccola district is smaller but equally enchanting. It offers a more intimate experience, with fewer tourists and a quieter ambiance. Here, you can explore the narrow alleyways, admire the intricate stone work, and perhaps even enter one of the trulli that have been converted into shops, cafes, or museums.

Locorotondo: Located just a short distance from Alberobello, the picturesque town of Locorotondo is another gem in the Puglian countryside. Locorotondo is renowned for its charming historic center, characterized by its circular layout and whitewashed houses with sloping roofs. As you wander through the narrow streets of Locorotondo, you'll notice the town's meticulous preservation of its traditional architectural style. The houses, painted in various shades of white, feature balconies adorned with colorful flowers, creating a delightful visual spectacle. Locorotondo's historical center is considered one of the most beautiful in Italy and has been recognized as a "Borghi più belli d'Italia" (Most Beautiful Villages of Italy). One of the highlights of Locorotondo is its central piazza, Piazza Vittorio Emanuele II. This charming square is the heart of the town and offers a perfect spot to relax and soak up the atmosphere. Surrounding the square, you'll find the Church of San Giorgio Martire, a striking example of baroque architecture. Locorotondo is also renowned for its excellent wine production, particularly its white wine made from the Verdeca grape variety. Visitors can explore the local vineyards, sample the delicious wines, and learn about the region's winemaking traditions. Both Alberobello and Locorotondo showcase the unique and captivating aspects of Puglian culture and architecture. Whether you are exploring the whimsical trulli or strolling through the circular streets of Locorotondo, these two destinations offer an unforgettable experience that will transport you to a bygone era of charm and beauty

Wine Tours in the Valle d'Itria

Wine tours in the Valle d'Itria region of Puglia offer a delightful experience for wine enthusiasts and travelers alike. Located in the southern part of Italy, Puglia is renowned for its rich viticultural heritage and picturesque landscapes. The Valle d'Itria, in particular, is a stunning area dotted with charming towns, rolling hills, and vineyards that produce some of Italy's finest wines.

During a wine tour in the Valle d'Itria, visitors have the opportunity to explore the unique characteristics of the region's wines, learn about the winemaking process, and indulge in tastings of exceptional local vintages. Here are some key highlights and features of wine tours in this enchanting part of Puglia:

Vineyard Visits: Wine tours in the Valle d'Itria typically include visits to local vineyards, where visitors can witness firsthand the beautiful grapevines and learn about the different grape varieties grown in the region. Experienced guides provide insights into the cultivation techniques, the influence of the local terroir, and the winemaking traditions that contribute to the unique flavors found in Valle d'Itria wines. Wine Tastings: Tasting sessions are a crucial component of any wine tour, and the Valle d'Itria offers a wide range of exceptional wines to sample. Visitors can savor aromatic white wines like Verdeca and Bianco d'Alessano, as well as robust reds such as Primitivo and Negroamaro. Additionally, the region is known for its delicious rosé wines, perfect for enjoying on warm summer days.

Trulli Experience: The Valle d'Itria is famous for its iconic trulli, traditional cone-shaped houses that are unique to the region. Many wine tours incorporate visits to vineyards located amidst picturesque trulli settlements, providing visitors with an immersive cultural experience alongside their wine exploration. The combination of stunning landscapes and traditional architecture adds an extra layer of charm to the tour.

Local Cuisine Pairings: Puglia is renowned for its exceptional cuisine, and wine tours often include food pairings that perfectly complement the local wines. Visitors can relish traditional dishes such as orecchiette pasta with tomato sauce, fresh seafood specialties, and delectable cheeses. The unique flavors of the region's culinary delights harmonize beautifully with the wines, enhancing the overall tasting experience.

Expert Guides: Knowledgeable guides accompany wine tours in the Valle d'Itria, offering valuable insights into the region's wine production, history, and cultural significance. They share stories about local winemakers, explain the characteristics of each wine tasted, and ensure that visitors have a memorable and educational experience.

Scenic Landscapes: The Valle d'Itria is characterized by its breathtaking landscapes, with rolling hills, vineyards, and olive groves as far as the eye can see. Wine tours often include leisurely walks through the picturesque countryside, allowing visitors to immerse themselves in the region's natural beauty and capture unforgettable moments.

Wine Festivals and Events: Depending on the time of year, visitors may have the opportunity to participate in local wine festivals and events. These celebrations showcase the best wines of the region and offer a vibrant atmosphere with live music, traditional dances, and cultural activities. It's a fantastic way to experience the lively spirit and warmth of the Valle d'Itria's wine culture.

Wine tours in the Valle d'Itria offer an unforgettable blend of wine, history, culture, and natural beauty. Whether you're a wine connoisseur or simply seeking a unique travel experience, exploring this picturesque region in Puglia will leave you with lasting memories and a deeper appreciation for Italian wines.

Printed in Great Britain
by Amazon

25406341R00126